12 Hidden Rewards of Making Amends

12
Hidden Rewards
of Making Amends

Finding Forgiveness and Self-Respect
by Working Steps 8–10

𝍦𝍦 𝍦𝍦 ||

ALLEN BERGER, PH.D.

HAZELDEN®

Hazelden
Center City, Minnesota 55012
hazelden.org

Library of Congress Cataloging-in-Publication Data

Berger, Allen, 1952-
   12 hidden rewards of making amends : finding forgiveness and self-respect by
working steps 8-10 / Allen Berger, Ph.D.
      pages cm
   Includes bibliographical references.
   ISBN 978-1-61649-446-9 (softcover) — ISBN 978-1-61649-494-0 (e-book)
1. Alcoholics—Rehabilitation. 2. Twelve-step programs. 3. Interpersonal relations.
4. Alcoholics—Family relationships. I. Title. II. Title: Twelve hidden rewards
of making amends.
   HV5278.B46 2013
   616.86'106—dc23

                                                                        2013007705

Editor's note
Some names, details, and circumstances have been changed to protect the privacy of those
mentioned in this publication.

This publication is not intended as a substitute for the advice of health care professionals.
Alcoholics Anonymous, AA, the Big Book, the *Grapevine, AA Grapevine,* and *GV* are registered
trademarks of Alcoholics Anonymous World Services, Inc.

The excerpts from *Twelve Steps and Twelve Traditions* and the text *Alcoholics Anonymous* are
reprinted with permission of Alcoholics Anonymous World Services, Inc. ("AAWS"). Permission
to reprint these excerpts does not mean that AAWS has reviewed or approved the contents of this
publication, or that AAWS necessarily agrees with the views expressed herein. A.A. is a program of
recovery from alcoholism only—use of these excerpts in connection with programs and activities
which are patterned after A.A., but which address other problems, or in any other non A.A. context,
does not imply otherwise.

24 23 22 21 20   2 3 4 5 6

Cover design: David Spohn
Interior design and typesetting: Madeline Berglund
Developmental editor: Peter Schletty

Dedication

This book is dedicated to William C. Rader, M.D., my first clinical supervisor, who taught me to trust my intuition and the value of authenticity in the client-counselor relationship. To Walter Kempler, M.D., my mentor in Gestalt therapy, who taught me the power of the present moment as the focal point of therapy, and how to confront someone and honor his or her dignity at the same time. To Tom McCall, my sponsor, who taught me the importance of being open, honest, and willing. To Bill B., who was my close friend and fellow traveler at the Kaneohe Marine Corps Air Station. And finally, this book is dedicated to my clients, who gave me the privilege of joining them on this sacred journey and who have helped me grow as a person and as a therapist.

Contents

Introduction

When you sit alone, quiet and free from distractions, are you at peace with yourself? Are you truly happy with how you are living your life? Are you deeply satisfied with how you behave in your relationships? Are you at peace with how you treat coworkers, friends, and family?

If you give yourself permission to be rigorously honest with yourself, and I mean gut-level honest with yourself, what happens? What comes into the foreground of your consciousness?

Most of us avoid this level of soul searching, this true-speaking and honest self-reflection. Why? Because we really don't want to feel our pain or our disappointment with ourselves. We don't want to face our dissatisfaction with ourselves. We don't want to admit that we aren't at peace with ourselves, that we are discontent with how we are living our lives.

None of us wants to admit that we've disappointed ourselves! So we avoid ourselves. We run away. We trick ourselves into believing that we are someone we aren't. We avoid facing ourselves honestly and openly. We believe that we are the fabricated-self that we have constructed to meet life's challenges.

Finding the courage to be rigorously honest would help us

develop the best possible attitude toward our relationship with ourselves, with others, and even with life itself. We would learn from our experiences and set upon the path of realizing our full human and spiritual potential. We would accept ourselves, support ourselves, and grow according to who we really are: our *true-self*. The true-self is purely you. It's the real you. Not the you that was altered by negative childhood experiences, not the you that was shaped by the anxiety about not belonging or not being loved or accepted, and not the you that was changed by our culture. It is the you that you were meant to be.

Unfortunately we rarely have the courage to face and deconstruct our *fabricated-self*, or *false-self*. The false-self or fabricated-self is a facade we use to disown our real feelings and manipulate our relationships with others. It's who we think we should be. It's who we think we need to be to relieve the pressure generated by the anxiety that we won't be loved or accepted. Our culture, our families, and even our own psyche conspire against our efforts, against taking this journey, against a gut-wrenching honesty. As M. Scott Peck (1978) pointed out in his book by the same name, this is the *road less traveled*.

The good news is that there are some pathfinders in our midst— people who have taken the road less traveled. They took it not because they possess some exceptional virtue in their character that we don't have; rather, they had to take that road or they would die.

I am referring to the millions of men and women who are in Twelve Step recovery. Their addiction induced a crisis that forced them to face themselves honestly. They reached a critical point in their lives that demanded change. They had to find a better way to live—or else! They were motivated to take certain steps to develop the best possible attitude toward themselves and life. They learned how to achieve real peace of mind and emotional well-being. They worked the Twelve Steps. Here are the Steps they took:

The Twelve Steps of Alcoholics Anonymous

Step 1: We admitted we were powerless over alcohol—that our lives had become unmanageable.

Step 2: Came to believe that a Power greater than ourselves could restore us to sanity.

Step 3: Made a decision to turn our will and our lives over to the care of God *as we understood Him.*

Step 4: Made a searching and fearless moral inventory of ourselves.

Step 5: Admitted to God, to ourselves, and to another human being the exact nature of our wrongs.

Step 6: Were entirely ready to have God remove all these defects of character.

Step 7: Humbly asked Him to remove our shortcomings.

Step 8: Made a list of all persons we had harmed, and became willing to make amends to them all.

Step 9: Made direct amends to such people wherever possible, except when to do so would injure them or others.

Step 10: Continued to take personal inventory and when we were wrong promptly admitted it.

Step 11: Sought through prayer and meditation to improve our conscious contact with God *as we understood Him,* praying only for knowledge of His will for us and the power to carry that out.

Step 12: Having had a spiritual awakening as the result of these steps, we tried to carry this message to alcoholics, and to practice these principles in all our affairs. (*Alcoholics Anonymous* 2001, 59–60)

We can learn from their lessons. We don't have to hit bottom or have a personal crisis to embrace change. We can take a similar journey because we choose to, because we want to, and because we are interested in reaching our potential. Because we want real peace of mind and serenity.

This book is for people who are new to the Twelve Steps as well as those who may be considered experienced pathfinders. For those new to the journey, I hope the book points you in an exciting and positive direction. For those who have walked many miles on the path, I hope you will gain a new perspective and see the Steps from a different angle.

If you are in recovery and working the Steps, I feel quite certain that I will be able to help you to better understand the therapeutic value of them. My goal, however, is more ambitious than just to promote an understanding of the psychological soundness of the Steps. I want to help you get past your "stuck points," to help you work through an impasse you might be experiencing in working the Steps, especially Steps 8, 9, or 10. I hope to help you become aware of your resistance and help you break through it.

The major focus of this book is on Steps 8, 9, and 10. I want to help you understand the twelve hidden rewards you will experience when you work these three Steps. First, let me define what I mean when I talk about hidden rewards. A hidden reward is an indirect benefit we receive from something helpful or therapeutic. Let's look at strength training as an example. While increasing strength is a direct benefit of this type of physical exercise, there are other indirect benefits. As lean muscle mass increases, our metabolic rate increases and we burn more calories. This increase in metabolism is a hidden reward of strength training.

We will see that there are twelve hidden rewards from working Steps 8, 9, and 10. While all twelve Steps are equally important, these three Steps are critical for achieving peace of mind and emotional well-being. As you will see, in order for us to experience peace of mind and serenity, we need to resolve the unfinished business in our lives by cleaning up the wreckage of our past. But that isn't enough. We also need to function according to a set of spiritual principles that will prevent us from doing more harm. Steps 8–10 guide us along this path. They help us develop the necessary skills to have healthier and more satisfying human relations. They help us reconcile our past, find forgiveness, and take the best possible attitude toward ourselves and others.

Let's put Steps 8–10 in context to better understand their significance. *The Twelve Step program is a design to ensure day-to-day emotional well-being and peace of mind.* Much work needs to be done, however, before the person in recovery reaches this phase of their development. They must deconstruct their reliance on a *false-self* and all that it demands they should be. They must deeply challenge themselves and their beliefs. They must hold themselves to a high level of accountability for their past actions and current behavior. They must ask for help. They also must go to any lengths to make these changes. It's quite an order, isn't it?

The Twelve Steps are a guide to recovering our lost true-self. They also create a more positive self-concept. Some people even describe the process of working the Steps as establishing "ego integrity." To realize the full benefit of the Twelve Steps, they must be worked in order because they are interdependent.

For example, the therapeutic forces unleashed when we take Step 1 create a powerful emotional and psychological energy that prepares us for what happens in Step 2. Step 1 is surrendering to reality. It is facing something about ourselves that we didn't want to face. When we face and accept reality without distorting it, a crisis results. In Step 1, we admit that we have a serious problem and we don't know what to do about it. We realize that we are between a rock and a hard place; we need a better solution but don't have one.

Step 2 tells us that there is a solution to our dilemma, that there is hope. This process is repeated throughout: Step 2 prepares us for Step 3, Step 3 for Step 4, and so on. A therapeutic momentum carries us along in the exact direction we need to go. This momentum forces us to confront the very issues that we have been avoiding and to develop the undeveloped parts of our personalities. It is a people-growing process. The Steps help us mature and grow a more positive self-concept and a more realistic view of ourselves and our life. This process exposes our false-self and creates more freedom from it, along with all the nonsense that goes along with living according to its ridiculous rules.

Later we will unpack the particular therapeutic value of each Step, but for now I want us to think of Steps 1–7 as a foundry that forges a key from honesty, open-mindedness, willingness, and self-awareness. That key unlocks a chest of hidden treasures: emotional sobriety, a positive self-concept, and an amazing inner force for growth, self-respect, trustworthiness, integrity, and wholeness. Many of us won't discover these hidden treasures because we balk at the difficult tasks inherent in Steps 8, 9, and 10.

What good is a key if we don't use it, if we just keep it in our pocket or let it dangle from our keychain? That's exactly the problem that many of us come across in recovery. We don't use the key we have forged in the first seven Steps because we want to avoid the discomfort we believe we are going to feel when we work Steps 8, 9, and 10. These are demanding Steps, no doubt about it. However, don't sell yourself short because of the erroneous belief that you can't handle the pain and discomfort.

If you don't hear anything else I say, I want you to hear this: *You are more capable than you realize.* Dr. Viktor Frankl made this observation as he was overseeing the care of men and women in a Nazi concentration camp: "We must never forget that we may also find meaning in life even when confronted with a hopeless situation, when facing a fate that cannot be changed" (1984, 116). He witnessed men and women deepen their spiritual life even under the most abhorrent conditions imaginable.

We have a wealth of untapped emotional and spiritual resources within that can help us face any challenge life puts in our path, even the most difficult, uncomfortable, and horrendous situations. There are those among us who have survived rape, molestation, concentration camps, genocide, prejudice, combat, torture, natural disasters, the loss of everything but life, or who have been witness to brutality and cruelty—the list goes on and on. The point is that we are resilient. If we weren't, we would no longer exist. We have an amazing ability to repair ourselves emotionally and to adapt. Unfortunately, many of us have never tapped into or used our ability to emotionally repair ourselves, so we don't even realize that this ability exists.

Researchers are discovering that infants aren't as fragile as we used to think, either (Tronick and Cohn 1989). They have a remarkable ability to soothe themselves when upset. However, what typically happens is that a loving parent intervenes and usurps the process. We, the parents, become anxious that the child is hurting and fear that he or she will be irreparably damaged, so we intercede to protect the child. When this happens, the child becomes dependent upon our intervention to create their well-being instead of using their inner resources to create their own state of emotional well-being. We create and reinforce emotional dependency rather than facilitate emotional resilience, and we do it all in the name of being a good parent. Unfortunately, we don't realize how competent children really are.

Perhaps our good intentions have contributed to the epidemic of codependency in our nation. We haven't learned how to take care of our emotional well-being. We look outside of ourselves for relief. We turn to drugs, love, sex, money, objects, work, or gambling to soothe our discontent or anxiety. We have become obsessed with and addicted to *more,* hoping that if we put enough into the emotional hole we will fill it. However, no one and no thing can fill that hole. Only *you* can fill it by learning how to soothe yourself.

If you commit yourself to the process of working Steps 8–10, you will open the door to your lost integrity and emotional resilience. You will be able to build a positive self-concept based on the reality of who you are (your true-self), rather than on some idealized image of who you think you should be but never can live up to (your false-self). You will build a way of living that works under any condition. You will develop self-respect and discover the healing powers of forgiveness.

Sounds like quite a promise, doesn't it? Well, it is. In fact, the founders of Alcoholics Anonymous (AA) understood the incredible power of this process and described the effects of working the Steps, which have been affectionately referred to as the "Promises." They guaranteed that if we worked the first nine Steps we would find a new freedom, peace of mind, and serenity.

What do Steps 8, 9, and 10 do? They help us take the necessary corrective actions to address the defects of character that were identified in the previous seven Steps. Steps 8–10 help us sort out guilt from shame, and sort out our real culpability from what we imagine. They help us understand forgiveness and compassion. These three Steps help us step up and take absolute responsibility for past and current behavior in the spirit of developing the best possible attitude we can take toward ourselves and others.

Steps 8, 9, and 10 help us achieve autonomy and emotional sobriety. Let's take a second look at them:

Step 8: Made a list of all persons we had harmed, and became willing to make amends to them all.

Step 9: Made direct amends to such people wherever possible, except when to do so would injure them or others.

Step 10: Continued to take personal inventory and when we were wrong promptly admitted it. (*Alcoholics Anonymous* 2001, 59)

You've Been Warned

I ask you to approach this work with an open mind and an open heart. I must warn you, however, that many dangers lie ahead. You will be asked to be honest with yourself in ways that most people avoid. It will not be easy, and it is not for the faint of heart. You will see things about yourself you won't like, but you will also discover things about yourself that will amaze you. You will see the worst in you and the best in you.

You will look at yourself through a very different lens. I will help you see *what is right* about you that you have alienated yourself from. You will see how you have twisted yourself into something you aren't in order to belong, to be loved and accepted, or to have power. This is what creates the real problem in your life. You will understand that you lost your true-self by seeking glory, that you betrayed your true-self to soothe your anxiety. You will see how you have sold out and lost your integrity. You will admit that you have betrayed friends and family because they have not submitted to your unreasonable expectations. With compassion for yourself in your heart, you will see how you settled for playing roles while living in constant fear that you were going to be found out.

Change begins when we accept who we are, rather than trying to be something we are not. You've heard it before: *the truth sets us free.* What most people haven't heard is that the truth will set us free *only if we are willing to live our truth.*

That's what this book is really about. It is going to provide you with a way of integrating your truth into your life. It will help you achieve autonomy and freedom from your psychic prison and all the nonsense you used to build your prison walls.

What You Need to Bring and What You'll Gain

I hope you will choose to take the risk and embrace the difficult road that lies ahead. If you do, then please make it your intention to be as present during this process as you can possibly be. Focus your attention on the thoughts and feelings that arise as you explore these issues. Think of your personal reactions as a signal from a light-house. Your reactions will illuminate where you need to go. If you remain open during this process, you will see what is missing in your life and what you need to do to remedy the problem.

Don't fret if you don't always understand what your reactions are telling you. Sometimes you will come to an "aha" immediately; other times it may take a day or more for a new path to emerge. The point is that if you begin this work, a process will take over that will lead you exactly where you need to go. I remind my patients of this often: "Trust the process." Later, you will learn more about what I mean by this statement.

I am very excited about sharing the wisdom of the Twelve Steps with you. By the time you finish reading this book and working with these principles, you will experience firsthand the value that these Steps can bring to your life. You will discover the soundness of the psychological principles at work in Twelve Step recovery and how to apply these in your life today—regardless of whether you suffer from an addiction.

Does it excite you to hear that you might be able to develop a deep sense of emotional well-being—to recover something important that you have lost? I hope it does, because I am excited to be your guide on this journey.

Before we unpack this process, I want to help you understand who you really are. I want to challenge your beliefs about your basic nature. I want to paint a picture of what it means to be a fully functioning person.

Part I:

Unpacking the Therapeutic Value
of the First Ten Steps and Some
Reflections on Working Steps 8–10

Chapter 1:
Who We Really Are: Wisdom and the Cycle of Experience

I don't know about you, but I am sick and tired of picking up a self-help book and being told what's wrong with me.

It's not that I am unwilling to look at my issues. (Well, OK, to be really honest, there have been times in my life when I've resisted facing my issues, but overall I do not.) It's that something doesn't feel right about the whole approach—that is, reducing a person to what's "wrong" in his or her life. We are all much more than what is wrong with us. We all have a desire to grow, to learn about ourselves, and to actualize ourselves. These basic needs are an important part of who we are, and these basic needs are awakened in recovery.

Until recently psychology was dominated by psychoanalytic and psychodynamic ideas. Psychoanalytic theory suggested that there was something innately wrong with us that needed fixing. Psychoanalysts argued that we suffered from a "repetition compulsion"; in other words, we are destined to act out our problems. They believed that our early childhood experiences created something similar to a groove in a record—a rut in our psyche that forces us to re-create the traumas we suffered in childhood. We are stuck replaying this tune for the rest of our lives. The theory is that in order to change, we need extensive treatment.

We have recently discovered that this is not true. Over the past seventy years, we have viewed our human nature in a very different way. Humanistic psychologists rejected the notion that something is innately wrong with us and instead put forth the idea that there is something inherently *right* about us. This way of thinking created a huge shift in the therapeutic community and suggested a novel way of relating to ourselves. Let's consider the psychoanalytic theory of "repetition compulsion." From a humanistic perspective we re-create these earlier traumas to work through our feelings and develop a part of ourselves that was hindered by the original traumas. Our basic need to grow and become whole motivates us to fill in what is missing in our personal development. With this new orientation in mind, our personal work or therapy has more to do with getting out of the way of our inner drive for self-realization than transforming our so-called uncivilized id into a good, productive citizen. (The id is a concept from psychoanalysis; Freud believed our mind could be divided into a superego or conscience, an ego, and an id. The id was the most primitive.) What ultimately makes us sick is ignoring our basic nature, not our basic nature per se. Let's explore this in more detail.

Right now, without being consciously aware of it, you are maintaining your internal body temperature at 98.6 degrees Fahrenheit. Your nervous system is programmed to keep your body temperature in a steady state or dynamic equilibrium called *homeostasis*. If you get cold, your nervous system will automatically do something to warm you up; for example, you might start shaking. If you get too hot, your nervous system will make you perspire to cool you off. It automatically responds to the change in your body temperature and makes the necessary adjustments until you return to normal. It's like we have a thermostat built into our nervous systems.

We automatically repair ourselves or regulate ourselves when something goes wrong with our temperature. This means that there is an incredible wisdom programmed into our nervous systems— just like flight is programmed into the nervous system of a bird. A bird does not have to be taught to fly. It just knows how to fly; once a fledgling's nervous system and body matures to a certain point, it takes off! It has an organic wisdom. We have such a wisdom too, as you will see.

The True-Self

We are each born with a true-self. Our true-self is like an acorn. According to Dr. Karen Horney, one of the unheralded geniuses in psychology, "You need not, and in fact cannot, teach an acorn to grow into an oak tree, but when given a chance, its intrinsic potentialities will develop" (1950, 17). Just like the acorn that is genetically programmed to become a unique oak tree, we are programmed to become our true-self (Horney 1950; Maslow 1962). Given the proper set of circumstances, we will develop the unique forces of our true-self—the ability to experience the depth of our own feelings, thoughts, wishes, desires, and needs. We will develop the faculty to express ourselves and spontaneously and respectfully relate to others. We will learn to equally honor our need for togetherness and our need to be ourselves. We will come to realize our own set of values and purpose in life. We will be able to tap our own resources to satisfy our needs and to regulate ourselves by soothing our pain or disappointment. We will develop a solid yet flexible self.

An acorn cannot reach its true potential unless it grows in a nurturing environment. The environment and climate have to provide certain critical elements. There needs to be an adequate amount of sunlight and water. The soil needs to contain certain nutrients. If these nutrient conditions are adequately met, then the acorn will eventually become what it is destined to be: a beautiful oak tree with a set of unique qualities and characteristics. However, the developing acorn cannot be exposed to harsh conditions until it is well rooted and has matured to a certain point.

The conditions for successful human development are very similar. Like the acorn, we have basic needs that must be satisfied for us to thrive. We need shelter, food, and water. We need a secure and warm attachment that will provide us with love and nurturing. We need intellectual and spiritual stimulation. We need encouragement and empathy. We need to be acknowledged and celebrated. We need to be protected from traumas and abuse. We also need some degree of healthy friction with the wishes and wills of others. If these conditions are adequately met, we will develop an inner security and an inner freedom that enables us to be response-able to our own feelings and express ourselves according to who we really are. Unfortunately, this rarely happens.

What Goes Wrong?

Through a variety of adverse influences, we do not grow according to our individual possibilities. A whole host of factors can easily distort our development: our desire to please, our need to belong or to be loved and accepted, incorrect learning, bad habits, anxiety, family dynamics, traumas, and cultural tradition.

We need to belong. We need love and acceptance to thrive emotionally and spiritually. So we are hardwired to seek it. The fear that we don't belong, that we won't be loved or accepted, creates a basic anxiety that permeates our lives. *This anxiety drives us to look for a solution that will ensure love and acceptance. Our anxiety makes us feel out of control, so we decide that we need to take control of our lives, and we head out on a quest to ensure love and acceptance.*

This path is called the "search for glory" (Horney 1950, 17). We search for a way of being that will ensure love and acceptance—that will make us feel like we belong. Our solution shapes our personality and beliefs. Here's what happens.

To solve the problem created by our basic anxiety, we develop a way of being that is based on an idealized image of who we think we should be. We believe this idealized-self will give us inner security. This is not our true-self. It is our false-self, or fabricated-self. (You can think of the false-self as our ego, as it is commonly referred to in the Twelve Step literature.)

In order for our idealized-self to crystallize into the false-self we must shape our personality accordingly. This is accomplished through our *pride system*. This system rewards and punishes us to ensure that we develop according to its idealized specifications or laws. We feel good and proud of ourselves when we act, behave, think, or feel the way we think we should (reward). We despise or even hate ourselves when we don't (punishment).

The laws and specifications of the pride system amount to a collection of "shoulds," which become a tyranny that exercises absolute control over our lives. We are driven to be the way our idealized image demands, and we dare not question its authority. These idealized specifications are absolutes; they are not negotiable. This in turn creates pervasive "black and white" thinking in our lives. Our false-self requires blind obedience. We do not question its tenets or its authority—we perceive it and feel it as the way we are supposed to be.

We sell out our true-self during this process. We sell out big time. We lose ourselves in this process, rejecting our true-self in favor of a fabricated false-self. We abandon and alienate ourselves from who we really are and become estranged from our true-self at a very deep level. Our anxiety leads us to believe that we aren't good enough the way we are and that to be OK, we must become something we are not. We develop a life based on phony aspirations. What a tragedy! We reject ourselves for an ideal. We swallow this solution whole and uncritically accept its nonsense.

To describe this process, I used the following analogy in *12 Smart Things to Do When the Booze and Drugs Are Gone.*

> Have you ever seen a beautiful bonsai tree? A bonsai artist works patiently over many years to constrain what should be a full-sized tree into perfect miniature. The artist constantly prunes the tree, wraps wires around its branches to shape them, deprives it of water, and trims its roots to fit a tiny pot. Such a tree becomes perfect to look at. And yet . . . and yet. It is not its true-self. It is a tree made to conform to a *vision* of miniature perfection. (2010, 26)

This is what we have done to ourselves with our "shoulds." They are the wire we wrap around our true-self to shape us into our idealized image.

Horney (1950) observed that our basic solution to our anxiety typically forms around three different unique themes that are developed outside of our consciousness:

- the *self-effacing* solution, based on the appeal of love
- the *expansive* solution, based on the appeal of mastery
- the *attitude of resignation,* based on the appeal of freedom

In all of these solutions, alienation from our true-self is the core problem.

If the *appeal of love* becomes the focus of our solution, we become self-effacing people pleasers. We feel inadequate, inferior, guilty, and contemptible. We must not think or feel superior to others or display any such feelings in our behavior lest we not be loved. Self-assertiveness makes us anxious. Therefore we can easily become victims in relationships. We dare not stand up for ourselves. We long for help, protection, and the experience of love both passionate and spiritual. We become chameleon-like, trying to figure out what someone wants us to be and molding ourselves to their image.

If the *appeal of mastery* becomes the focus of our solution, we try to get love and acceptance via the expansive solution. We earn love by excelling, by being the best, and by being superior in some way. This is the opposite of the self-effacing solution. If we follow the appeal of mastery, we tend to manipulate or dominate others to make them dependent upon us. We strive for power over others, either through becoming superior or by being ruthlessly vindictive. We identify with our idealized image and become arrogant and narcissistic.

Finally, if the *appeal of freedom* attracts us, then we will withdraw from the inner battlefield and declare ourselves uninterested. This is the attitude of resignation: we resign from the so-called rat race. This is the most radical of all the solutions. We give up and stop trying. We become indifferent underachievers. We are seen as having all kinds of potential, but no ambition or desire for success.

You are likely to recognize one of these three themes in your life. We all develop along one of these paths, essentially rejecting our true-self. What we didn't realize at the time we rejected ourselves is that *any life based on self-rejection will never be fulfilling or satisfying.*

The Price We Pay

The pain and trauma caused by the alienation from our true-self manifests in a myriad of symptoms, including alcoholism and other drug addictions. Dr. Carl Jung believed that this alienation actually caused alcoholism. In a letter to Bill Wilson, Jung stated that the alcoholic had a "spiritual thirst" (Wilson 1988a, 280). He went on to explain that the alcoholic had a longing to be whole and one with God and that the effects of alcohol and other drugs simulated the experience, leading many to return to it repeatedly.

I believe we long to be united with our real-self. This is what creates wholeness and integrity. This is the path to a real connection with a "God of our understanding."

Abandoning our true-self sets in motion a juggernaut of absurd behaviors aimed at satisfying the unyielding demands of our false-self, with its system of rigid laws and perfectionistic specifications. When this juggernaut couples with alcoholism, addiction to other drugs, and/or a process addiction (such as sex, gambling, video games, shopping, or stealing), the result is devastating.

We are not destined to stay on this fabricated path. Something inside us desires self-realization and self-actualization. Something deep inside yearns for us to be who we really are. We desire wholeness and integrity.

We can deconstruct our false-self and begin living a more meaningful and fulfilling life right now. Our true-self is never permanently removed. Famed humanistic psychologist Abraham Maslow (1954) stated that our basic needs are "intrinsic aspects of human nature which culture cannot kill, but only repress." They are there for our discovery; they are there to be recovered.

The Nature of the True-Self

What is the nature of our true-self? I have pondered this question for most of my career as a psychologist. The following is my best answer to this question. Let us begin understanding our true nature by becoming aware that we possess a very powerful growth force called self-actualization. This force is hardwired into our DNA.

Maslow determined that we demonstrate in our own nature a pressure toward fuller and fuller being and that we grow toward a more and more perfect actualization of our humanness in exactly the same naturalistic, scientific sense that an acorn may be said to be "pressing toward" being an oak tree (Goble 1971, 38). This drive toward self-realization remains a part of us. It lies dormant within. *When we remove the destructive forces of our addictions and our false-self, the constructive forces of the real-self are reintroduced into our lives and facilitate our growth and self-actualization.* We are propelled toward self-realization.

Who are we when we actualize our human potential? How will we behave? How do we function when we transcend our false-self? We must answer these questions to understand the self we are recovering by working the Twelve Steps.

This will sound strange, but the healthy person doesn't have much personality. This doesn't mean that they are bland or boring. Quite the contrary. It means that they do not respond to a situation in a stereotyped or rigid manner. A healthy person is flexible and focused on the current moment. A healthy person uses their full awareness and intuition to invent how to respond appropriately to a novel situation or to satisfy their needs. A healthy person makes *creative adjustments* to their environment to satisfy their needs.

Our true-self is response-able, which means that we are not identified with any self-configuration. Our true-self isn't one self, but a population of selves working in harmony. This idea may sound strange to you because we tend to think of the true-self as one self, but it isn't. Don't be alarmed—this doesn't mean we have a Sybil-like multiple personality disorder. It means that when we are functioning from our true-self we can respond from any part of our self that would help restore our homeostasis, by either eliminating tension or gratifying a need. We adopt a way of being that is appropriate to the life situation we are facing. When we are real, when we are authentic, we function spontaneously. We tap our inner wisdom, and we learn to trust ourselves as never before. We learn to make creative adjustments.

Carl Rogers (1961), often considered the father of humanistic psychology, felt that the person who is psychologically free behaves in the following ways:

- He is more able to live fully in and with each and all of his feelings and reactions.
- She makes increasing use of all of her ability to sense accurately the existential situation within herself and in her environment.
- He makes use of the information his nervous system supplies, using it in awareness, but recognizing that his intuition may be, and often is, wiser than his awareness.
- She is more able to function freely and select from the multitude of possibilities the behavior that in this moment of time will be most generally and genuinely satisfying.
- He is able to put more trust in his functioning, not because he is infallible, but because he can be fully open to the consequences of his actions and correct them if they prove to be less than satisfying.
- She is more able to experience all of her feelings, and is less afraid of any of her feelings.
- He is his own sifter of evidence, and therefore is open to input from all sources.
- She is completely engaged in the process of being and becoming herself.
- He lives more completely in this moment, and knows that this is the soundest living for all time.

- She is becoming a more fully functioning organism, and because of the awareness of herself that flows freely in and through her experience, she is becoming a more fully functioning person. (191–92)

When we operate from our real-self, we have a solid but flexible sense of self. We honor ourselves, support ourselves, and take responsibility to satisfy our needs—*but only if we don't get in our own way.* The path we follow to satisfy our needs or eliminate tension is called the *cycle of experience.* Let's explore this in more detail.

The Cycle of Experience

What happens when we are hungry but don't have time to eat before we drive home from work? Our need to satisfy our hunger moves into the foreground of our consciousness until it's satisfied. It creates a disequilibrium that motivates us to satisfy the unmet need. If the route home takes us on the freeway, we will notice all the billboards advertising places to eat. We spontaneously seek out the things in our environment that will satisfy our hunger. Once we eat and satisfy our hunger, we will hardly notice those advertisements that seemed so compelling just moments earlier. This is an example of the innate wisdom that motivates us and orients our senses to the relevant information in our environment so we can satisfy our needs or eliminate tension.

But what is it that makes us function in this manner? Underlying our behavior is a process called *self-regulation.* Very simply stated, we strive to maintain a balance between need gratification and tension elimination. A healthy person identifies his or her most meaningful need and responds to it appropriately, thereby restoring balance (peace of mind), releasing new energy, and allowing the next important need to emerge. Self-regulation is obtained by moving through various stages of the cycle of experience.

To illustrate the cycle of experience, let's look at what happens when we need to eliminate the tension caused by the urge to urinate. Follow along in figure 1.

Figure 1. Cycle of Experience

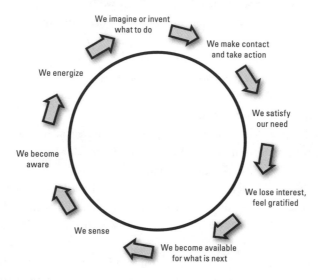

Your bladder is constantly filling with urine (We sense). When the volume of urine reaches a certain level, we become aware of the need to void the urine (We become aware). The next thing that happens is we mobilize ourselves to eliminate the tension caused by the urine in our bladder (We energize). We search our environment to find a restroom and head straight for it (We imagine or invent what to do). Once we do what we need to do in the restroom (We make contact and take action), the tension caused by a full bladder is eliminated (We satisfy our need) and we stop thinking about urinating (We lose interest). Once our need to urinate is eliminated, we become available for whatever comes next. This is how the cycle operates to address a physical need. Next, we will look at what happens with a psychological tension.

Let's imagine Jeremy had an argument with his spouse the other day, and ever since then something has been gnawing at him (We sense). He just doesn't feel good about what happened. Jeremy wasn't able to identify what was bothering him, but after he thought about it for a while he realized that he needed to make amends (We become aware). He said many things that he doesn't feel good about. He needs to apologize, to work Step 10. Yesterday, he didn't think his partner deserved an apology. He justified his rotten behavior. Today, he realized that there is no justification for talking to someone he cares about in that way. That is not the person he wants to be.

Once Jeremy became aware of what he wanted, he mobilized himself to take action. He energized himself to take action and reached out to his wife to discuss his real feelings (We imagine or invent what to do). He ended up saying:

> "Hon, are you available to talk with me about our conversation yesterday? I want to apologize for what I said to you and how I justified my actions. I am sorry, truly sorry for calling you names and then justifying my behavior. You didn't deserve to be treated that way. I was upset with myself and took it out on you. Is there something I can do to repair the damage I've done to you? You don't deserve to be treated that way. I am sorry. I plan on talking to my sponsor about my anger."

Sometimes making amends unfolds differently than expected. Let's imagine that Jeremy started to cry unexpectedly. As he made amends, he realized that the way he had treated his wife was similar to how he was treated as a child. This was what his father, now deceased, used to do to him when his father was upset with himself.

Jeremy learned this abusive behavior at his father's feet. Jeremy's unresolved pain surfaced during his discussion with his wife. To address this unresolved trauma, he needs to follow a different path.

A fully functioning person will be willing and able to follow the path of their experience wherever that path leads. In the example above, Jeremy will need to address his feelings toward his father, once he has finished making amends to his wife. Because his father passed away, he may need to imagine his dad sitting in front of him while he says the things to him he has always wanted to say about being mistreated. Here's an example of something one of my patients shared with me the other day.

About two weeks ago, Sharon's father passed away. He had been ill for several months, and his death was expected. Sharon had come to peace about his passing and spent a wonderful day with him on Father's Day. She sat at his bedside, cared for him, talked to him, and let him know how much she loved him. He passed away two days after she flew back home.

The funeral and wake was scheduled for Saturday. Sharon was going to take the red-eye flight and arrive in New Jersey around 8 a.m. Her stepmother, Eleanor, scheduled the funeral and wake for 10 a.m. When Sharon found out the time, she called Eleanor and asked if she'd be willing to reschedule the services to later in the day, giving her time to freshen up and get settled in to her hotel. Eleanor flat-out refused. This was one of many conflicts that Sharon had experienced with her stepmother—she was always unwilling to accommodate her stepdaughter's needs. Sharon was furious. She went out on her back porch and started yelling at her stepmother, even though she was not actually there, telling her how frustrated she was with her selfishness and her disrespect. Sharon's tirade lasted twenty-five minutes and was very cathartic.

This cycle of sensing and acting to heal a negative inner

experience is how we function when we *don't* get in our own way. Unfortunately, many of us are not this spontaneous or free to flow with our experience. Instead we turn to others to soothe us or we try to deny our needs, which interrupts the cycle of experience. For example, if Sharon had been raised with the idea "If you don't have something nice to say, don't say anything at all," she likely would have stopped herself from getting angry. She would have internalized her feelings.

Our false-self interrupts our ability to flow with our experience. If, according to our false-self, a need arises that we shouldn't have, we won't acknowledge it or we won't respond to it. If our false-self doesn't recognize a need, we won't energize or mobilize ourselves to take the action required to eliminate it or satisfy it. If our false-self is afraid to let go of something, we won't release it. As you can see in figure 2, we can disrupt or block the cycle of experience at any point in the transition from one stage to the next.

Figure 2. Interrupted Cycle of Experience

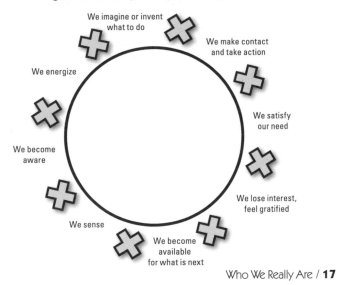

We imagine or invent
what to do

We make contact
and take action

We energize

We satisfy
our need

We become
aware

We lose interest,
feel gratified

We sense

We become
available
for what is next

Our ability to flow with or follow our cycle of experience is restored in recovery. Even more to the point, Steps 8–10 are crucial in restoring self-regulation and in creating true peace of mind.

We have a need to complete unfinished business. Erving and Miriam Polster, two acclaimed Gestalt therapists, observed that "all experience hangs around until a person is finished with it" (1973, 36). Unfinished business is stored in the background of our consciousness, waiting for an opportunity to come forward for resolution. The more unfinished business we have stored up, the harder it is for us to function in the present moment. These unfinished issues demand our attention and divert our psychological resources. Each issue we resolve frees up psychological resources, which we can then use to get on with living and actualizing our potential.

The process is quite simple, but never easy. What this means for us is that to achieve peace of mind and emotional freedom, we need to complete our unfinished business and be responsive to our needs. I like to refer to this as being response-able. Being response-able is at the heart of Steps 8, 9, and 10.

The remarkable thing about the Twelve Steps is that they help us recover our lost true-self. They help us restore our authenticity and our ability to flow with our experience. They restore self-realization, which in turn restores our self-actualization. It is truly an incredible program, as you are about to see in the next chapter.

Chapter 2:
Unpacking the Therapeutic Effects of the Twelve Steps

The Twelve Steps of Alcoholics Anonymous have been heralded as the most important spiritual development of the past 100 years (Rohr 2011). It is my opinion that they should also be considered one of the most innovative psychological interventions of the past century. As evidence, consider the fact that the Twelve Steps have had more success in treating a wide variety of addiction problems than all other medical or psychological intervention or treatment programs combined (Schenker 2009).

What are the therapeutic forces that enable the Twelve Steps to help so many people who are struggling to reclaim their lives? My conclusion is that the Twelve Steps help us recover our lost true-self. They provide a framework that helps us work out a new understanding of ourselves and that teaches us a design for living that encourages authenticity and responsibility. This new design for living honors our basic nature. Working the Twelve Steps creates a powerful personal transformation that leads to a deep sense of well-being, serenity, and peace of mind.

As you learned in the previous chapter, a main source of much of our psychological distress stems from the belief that we need to be something we aren't—that is, attempting to live by the unreasonable demands of our false-self. We have alienated ourselves from our true-self in favor of an idealized version of who we should be. We've lost sight of the importance of character, people-centered values, keeping our integrity, authenticity and honesty, and honoring our true-self. We've made things more important than people.

This is the veer in the trajectory of our personal development that the Twelve Steps correct. The Steps help us wake up from the trance that our culture has created. They help us deconstruct our reliance on a false-self and guide us on an incredible journey of self-discovery and self-actualization. They help us clean house and make amends to those people we have hurt. They help us stay centered, grounded, and humble. They help us become authentic and present in our lives. They help us restructure our self-concept into something more positive, solid, and flexible. They help us recover our true-self.

Abraham Maslow (1962, 22) made the following observations about the importance of a basic need like self-actualization:

- The absence of self-actualization breeds illness. (The absence of our true-self creates serious problems; it becomes a breeding ground for addictions and other forms of psychopathology.)
- The presence of our true-self prevents illness. (This is the most important protective factor against alcoholism and other drug addictions.)
- The restoration of the true-self cures illness. (This is the experience millions of us have had in recovery: our true-self is restored through working the Twelve Steps.)

In the next two chapters I will explore the changes that take place within us during the process of working the first seven Steps, but before I do, let's look at how the Twelve Steps are organized.

The Organization of the Twelve Steps

The Twelve Steps are numbered for good reason. The optimal therapeutic benefit occurs when they are worked in order, because the Steps are interdependent. As I mentioned before, each Step builds on the one that precedes it to create a powerful transformative experience. What happens in Step 1 creates an experience that readies a space in our psyche for what happens in Step 2. Step 2 leads to what happens in Step 3, and so on. This is how change unfolds across all Twelve Steps. The Twelve Steps create a momentum that motivates us to honestly face ourselves and others like we have never done before.

Grouping the Steps

We can cluster or group the Twelve Steps into four functional groups. Steps 1–3 form the first grouping. These Steps demolish the foundation of our self-destructive life, the one that didn't work, and build a stronger and more resilient foundation for a new life that works under any condition whatsoever.

Steps 4–7 form the second grouping. These Steps help us develop a positive self-concept by encouraging authenticity and promoting self-awareness and personal accountability. They help us to become our best possible selves.

The third grouping, which consists of Steps 8 and 9, helps us become trustworthy by righting the wrongs we have done to others. They teach us the nature of healthy relationships and to aim at having the best possible attitude toward human relations.

The last three Steps, Steps 10–12, form the final cluster. These

Steps help us maintain our new way of life. They continue to promote self-awareness, self-realization, and emotional maturation through serving others and an ongoing program of personal and spiritual growth. These groupings are summarized in Table 1.

Table 1. Summary of the Organization of the Twelve Steps

Group	Steps	Purpose
I	1–3	Build the foundation for our personal transformation, for our recovery.
II	4–7	Help us develop a positive self-concept by encouraging authenticity, increasing our self-awareness, and promoting responsibility and accountability.
III	8 and 9	Help us become trustworthy by righting the things we have done wrong to others, and teach us about the nature of healthy relationships.
IV	10–12	Help us maintain and deepen our humility and the connection to our true-self, as well as expand and enrich our consciousness, through serving others.

The process of working the Steps is like constructing a building from the ground up. You'd work in intervals and wouldn't move on until the previous job was completed. First, you'd demolish the old foundation because it was faulty, weak, and unable to support the new structure you hoped to build. Next, you'd dig a foundation and strengthen it with mortar and steel, and then you'd build the frame. In the meantime, you would constantly provide necessary maintenance to keep what you already built in good shape. In construction, it's essential to use the best talent and materials available. You wouldn't build something halfheartedly. And so it is with working the Steps. The Steps must be worked to the best of our abilities if we are to gain their full benefits.

The Steps facilitate a restructuring of the self. They help us find meaning in our lives and in our recovery by changing our emotional and spiritual values. Before we focus on the process of making amends and the twelve hidden rewards that follow, I want to spell out in some detail the therapeutic effects of working the first seven Steps. It's important that we understand the changes that take place within us when we work the first seven Steps. If it were not for the work we do in Steps 1–7, we would be hard-pressed to make a list of those we have harmed, make amends to them when appropriate, and develop a practice of self-reflection that leads to self-regulation.

After we explore what happens to us when we work the first seven Steps, we will delve into Steps 8, 9, and 10. I will help you understand the therapeutic effects of these three Steps and the issues worth considering while working them. I want to help you see exactly what happens to us when we deconstruct a life that doesn't work and then construct a new life that does work under any condition whatsoever.

Let's now turn to the beginning of this powerful transformative process, Step 1.

Chapter 3:
Unpacking the
Therapeutic Value
of Steps 1-3

The first three Steps help us demolish the foundation on which we built a life that ultimately led to our demise. They help us begin to build a healthier foundation. They give us hope that a better life is possible, that we can become our best possible self, and that we can build a stronger and more resilient foundation for a new life that works under any condition whatsoever.

Let's now turn to the task of unpacking these first three Steps and learn how they initiate a powerful process of personal transformation and change.

Step 1: We admitted we were powerless over alcohol—that our lives had become unmanageable.

Therapeutic Effect: Shatters the illusion of control, undermines our reliance on our false-self, and induces an existential crisis.

We must unhook our dependence upon our false-self if we are to recover our lost true-self and build a better, more flexible, stronger, and more resilient foundation for our lives.

Let's not kid ourselves: this is quite an order. Our false-self was adopted to resolve the anxiety stemming from our concern that we wouldn't be loved or accepted. This anxiety created a powerful force that shaped our personality and drove the formation of a false-self: a self that was based on an idealized version of who we should be. We became driven to obey its commands.

It has always struck me as ironic that we tried to take control of our lives by adopting a false-self as the solution to our anxiety, when in reality we lost control of our lives—of our true-self. This is especially ironic for the alcoholic and the addict, who possess a defiant self-reliance. We hate being told what to do by anyone or anything, and yet we lost complete control of ourselves and gave that control to our false-self.

Our idealized-self was shaped by many different factors, but primarily by our family dynamics (which rarely encourage the development of the true-self) and by our cultural values and norms. One family task is to communicate its cultural norms and values to children. Our culture values success, having power, having control, having things, and having independence. It's been described as a culture based on "having."

The nature of our culture influenced the traits we selected to construct our idealized-self. The traits that were related to "having" became highly valued, while their opposites were not. Therefore helplessness and powerlessness and ignorance were judged as deplorable, shameful, and undesirable traits. These characteristics were unacceptable because we believed that we would never belong nor be loved nor accepted if we were helpless, powerless, ignorant, or unsuccessful. Our idealized-self rejected these traits, and they became our despised-self—the self we want to bury, that we hope no one will ever discover. Our despised-self therefore possesses all the traits and behaviors that our false-self deems unacceptable or unattractive. The irony is that we all have a despised-self, and it contains the same things we keep hidden from one another: that which ultimately connects us all in our humanity is hidden, rejected, despised, and disowned.

Our idealized-self is clearly based on the notion of having power and being in control, not on being powerless. We attempt to achieve emotional security by controlling how people think and feel about us. We try to control what we think or feel and how we behave to manipulate others into thinking we are our false-self. Power and control are the names of the games that our false-self plays. When someone or something comes along and tries to take control away from us, it feels like someone is trying to remove something we need for our survival.

After working with alcoholics and observing their behavior, Tamerin and Neumann (1974) described the problem in this way:

> If he were less of a perfectionist, less preoccupied with the need to control himself, less concerned with the opinion of others, and more able to tolerate his limitations, accepting the fact of his alcoholism might be an easier task. But to acknowledge one's alcoholism is often to feel defective and inferior. (15)

No wonder we have so much difficulty getting clean and sober. Our false-self defines needing help as being defective and inferior.

It's a spiritual axiom that the more we try to control our lives, the more we lose control. This is at the heart of Step 1: we are being asked to admit our powerlessness. Bill Wilson described it quite accurately in *Twelve Steps and Twelve Traditions* (1981) when he wrote, "Every natural instinct cries out against the idea of personal powerlessness" (21). For us, control is essential to our well-being, even though in reality the opposite is true.

Recovery begins when the personal myth of control is shattered. We give up controlling our lives and stop trying to control others; we stop trying to control our drinking or drug use or whatever we are trying to control. We accept and surrender to the reality that we are out of control. This is the crack in our cosmic egg that begins the deconstruction of our false-self. Bill Wilson described this process as "deflation at depth." It has also been referred to as "hitting bottom" (Tiebout 1999, 13).

Dr. Harry Tiebout (1999), one of the first psychiatrists to endorse Alcoholics Anonymous, talked about the importance of shattering the alcoholic's ego (which is really the same as the false-self):

> It was this ego that had to become humble. Then the role of hitting bottom, which means reaching a feeling of personal helplessness, began to be clear. It was this process that produced in the ego an awareness of vulnerability, initiating the positive phase. In hitting bottom the ego becomes tractable and is ready for humility. The conversion experience has started. (31)

Hitting bottom dispels the personal myth of control and shatters our reliance on the false-self, which in turn creates the possibility to discover who we really are.

When we surrender, our reliance on our false-self is weakened. This is critical to the foundation of our recovery, and it is what is meant in the line "little good can come to any alcoholic who joins A.A. unless he has first accepted his devastating weakness and all its consequences" (*Twelve Steps and Twelve Traditions* 1981, 21).

An analogy might help us understand what happens next. Let's suppose we don't know how to swim, and we are out in deep, stormy seas clinging desperately to our soggy life preserver. If we let go, we fear we are going to drown. Therefore we cling to this life preserver, even though it has become waterlogged and does not work well. If we keep clinging to it we are eventually going to drown.

We cling to our false-self in the same way. We hold on to it just like we cling to that soggy, ineffective life preserver. When a counselor, therapist, or sponsor in AA or Narcotics Anonymous (NA) comes along and tells us, "Let go of the life preserver, you won't drown! I'll help you, take my hand. Trust me!" our first response is disbelief: "You've got to be kidding me! I'm not letting go of this life preserver. It's all I have!"

Step 1 teaches us about the paradoxical nature of the process of change. Change is not straightforward. A paradox turns reality on its head; it is the opposite of what we assume. "Change occurs when a person becomes what he is, rather than when he tries to become what he is not" (Beisser 1970, 77). We need to admit our dilemma, to find a solution. We need to let go, to live and get control over our lives. We need to surrender to win; and ultimately, we need to admit and accept our powerlessness, to discover a better source of power—a higher power—a power greater than our false-self.

Surrendering puts us in quite a pickle, doesn't it? We have spent our lives trying to control ourselves and others, and everything else in our lives. By surrendering, we are relinquishing that control—we are letting go. This creates an *existential crisis.* The essence of this crisis is that we have let go of our dependence upon our false-self and upon drugs but have nothing new to replace it. We are in limbo; we are in a personal crisis.

The instant we surrender and become honest with ourselves, we see clearly that we can't drink or use again and that we have made a mess of things—our experience proves this. When we face our personal limitations, an existential crisis emerges. We are powerless, helpless, and hopeless. There is nothing left to hold on to, and nothing left to do.

Surrender is critical to recovery. It becomes the "firm bedrock upon which happy and purposeful lives may be built" (*Twelve Steps and Twelve Traditions* 1981, 21). This existential crisis creates a desperation that fuels the process of change. Don't run from this crisis and the pain that it engenders. It is the key that opens the door to recovery and opens your heart and mind to a new way of life.

Remember, the Twelve Steps are interdependent. This is why it is necessary to enter recovery through a personal crisis, through this existential crisis. This crisis creates an emotional state of hopelessness that prepares us for Step 2. It opens our hearts and minds to this powerful transformative process we call recovery. Let's see what Step 1 has prepared us for in Step 2.

Step 2: Came to believe that a Power greater than ourselves could restore us to sanity.

Therapeutic Effect: Instills hope.

Surrender caused an existential crisis. We felt broken, defeated and hopeless. We begrudgingly accepted the harsh reality that our current thinking just wasn't going to cut it. We failed; our original solution to life was being deconstructed. We needed something, anything. We needed hope.

Hope is critical at this juncture. Hope gives us the belief that things can be different, that there is more to life than our false-self has led us to believe. Hope is the belief that a better solution is within our grasp.

It turns out that hope is a common factor in all types of healing. Research conducted by Dr. Jerome Frank (1963) helped us understand the importance of hope. He compared four very different approaches to healing human suffering: (1) traditional Western medicine, (2) religion and religious conversion experiences, (3) shamans, and (4) psychotherapy. He searched for the commonality among these different approaches and found that the active ingredient, or the therapeutic force, in all of them was *hope*.

Hope is mobilized through four factors:

- a special healing setting
- a rationale, myth, or conceptual framework that explains the problem and a method for resolving it
- an emotionally charged, confiding relationship with a helping person
- a ritual or procedure that requires involvement of both the healer and the client to effect a "cure" or resolution

These four factors can also be found in the Twelve Step program.

A Special Healing Setting

The authentic nature of the Twelve Step fellowship creates a unique atmosphere for people to change. I remember when I attended my first meeting over forty-one years ago. At that meeting, a young man named Tom M. shared about his experiences with alcohol and other drugs. He told us how his journey in recovery began. He spoke of wanting to belong but never feeling a part of life. He revealed his personal insecurities with women. He discussed how crazy it felt to be an egomaniac with low self-esteem. He talked openly about his sense of inadequacy. I had never seen a man so open and honest with his feelings: I was blown away! I loved this kind of raw authenticity, this true-speaking. It satisfied a hunger for truth and honesty I had, but rarely honored. What impressed me was how open and honest he was about things that I felt but never wanted anyone to know. I wouldn't even admit these feelings to myself.

He willingly removed his social mask and related to us from his innermost self. He wasn't playing games or trying to look good or make a good impression. He was being himself, true-speaking and discussing things that I would have never dreamed of sharing even with a close friend, let alone with a group of strangers. Tom was free to be himself.

The only way I could achieve this kind of inner peace and personal freedom was when I was drinking or using. Then and only then was I free from the fears and insecurities that crippled my ability to be present and enjoy life. What moved me was that Tom had found a path to creating personal freedom in the Twelve Step fellowship by working the Twelve Steps. There was something magical going on, and I wanted to be a part of it. It may sound strange to you, but this was the first time in my life that I felt like I belonged.

Tom became my sponsor, and he continues to sponsor me today. We have trudged the path of recovery together for more than forty-one years. Tom is three years ahead of me on this journey. I have grown to love him and respect him for who he is and all that he has done to help the addict who still suffers. I will be forever grateful to him.

I'll discuss the nature of our relationship later, but for now I want you to know that Twelve Step meetings provide a very special and safe place to heal. These meetings are based on authenticity, on owning shortcomings, and on sharing our experience, strength, and hope. They are based on working together toward the primary purpose of the group.

I hope you are getting a sense of the special climate in the Twelve Step fellowships. This climate encourages us to face ourselves as we are, and to own our mistakes and grow from them. It's a very powerful atmosphere. The effect the group had on me was to fill me with hope and a belief that I could achieve personal freedom from my inner fears and insecurities without using alcohol and other drugs. Hearing Tom that summer night in 1971 unlocked the door to a new reality, to a new life—a life full of possibilities and free from alcohol and other drugs.

A Rationale That Explains the Problem and a Method for Resolving It

The rationale that AA provided me to understand my problem with alcohol and other drugs saved my life. It gave me a way of confronting my problems without losing face. It provided me with an explanation of my problem that permitted me to keep my dignity. When I was told that I suffered from a medical disease that consisted of a physical allergy coupled with a mental obsession, I was able to forgive myself enough for the horrible things that I had done, to myself and others, to begin the process of recovery.

I realized that I suffered from a disease. I wasn't a bad person needing to become good; I was physically, emotionally, and spiritually sick, needing help. What a relief! This gave me hope that I could be healed, that my life could be free from the chains of addiction and all the insanity that was associated with it. It kept my false-self off my back enough for me to support my efforts in recovery.

AA also provided me with a healing road map. I was also told that "rarely have we seen a person fail who has thoroughly followed our path" (*Alcoholics Anonymous* 2001, 58). This meant that there was a method for recovering from addiction. There were steps— Twelve Steps—that I could take to give me a design for living that would set me free. I was all in. I wanted a better life, and I was given a recipe for achieving it. There was hope!

An Emotionally Charged, Confiding Relationship with a Helping Person

My relationship with Tom M. saved my life. He was the first person I trusted enough to be completely honest with. Tom's acceptance of me as I was, warts and all, created a very safe climate for me to share with him my darkest secrets. I didn't have to impress him by pretending I was someone I wasn't. What impressed him the most was me being myself—being my actual-self, openly and honestly.

Lest I create the wrong impression that this was a one-way street, I want you to know that it wasn't. Far from it. Tom's willingness to share his darkest secrets was also a factor in my allegiance to him. He walked like he talked; he wasn't a hypocrite. He lived by the principles he was advocating. He struggled to integrate them into his life and humbly shared his difficulty, openly and honestly. He taught me that recovery was a process, not an event—that this wasn't a 100-yard dash, but a marathon that would be grueling at times. That we strove for progress, not perfection.

This was the first time in my life that I had a relationship with another human being that was based on acceptance and positive regard. Tom saw a self in me that I could only hope was there. He had faith in me when I didn't; he saw possibilities where I saw none. He loved me until I could start loving myself. Ours was an emotionally charged relationship that awakened a hope and belief that I could heal from my disease. He helped me see that there was much more to me than my addiction. I am forever grateful for his loving presence in my life.

The Twelve Step fellowship provides an emotionally charged, confidential, and loving relationship—both with fellow members of the program and through a very special relationship with a sponsor.

A Procedure That Requires the Involvement of Both the Healer and the Client to Effect a Cure

Tom encouraged me to work the Twelve Steps. He emphasized how crucial the Steps were to recovery and said I could find the solution to my problems in them. This was the procedure he recommended, and I followed his direction. I couldn't have done it alone. He sat with me as we read and discussed each Step in depth. We looked at how the content related to me and what it had to teach me about my addiction and the path I needed to take to recover. After these personal, intense, and insightful discussions, he would instruct me to write, to journal my response to the tasks suggested in each Step. After I completed these writing assignments, I read the results to him as he listened intently. He consistently offered me very helpful comments, some of which I didn't like. Because I trusted him, I could accept his criticism and work through my defensiveness. Together, we were reconstructing my life by challenging my personal myths and "stinking thinking." We were restoring my wholeness. He was helping me extract my true-self from the tangled knots of my false-self.

Working the Steps requires the involvement of both the sponsor and the sponsee. My relationship with Tom reinforced my growing belief that there was hope. My cynicism was slowly dying, and I could clearly see changes taking place in my life. I was on the road to recovery.

Step 1 had us admit our powerlessness. We realized that we can't lick this problem on our own. Step 2 tells us there is a solution, that with help we can find a way out of this mess. *Step 2 generates hope.* Hope resolves our existential crisis.

Step 2 also continues to deconstruct the false-self. The solution to our problems needs to be found in a new state of consciousness, not in the consciousness conceived by the false-self. We are taught in the program that we cannot solve a problem with the consciousness that created it. We cannot continue to follow the edicts of our false-self if we are going to recover.

This restructuring of the self is at the heart of the therapeutic value of the Twelve Steps. We have to deconstruct our reliance on our false-self to recover our true-self. Hope tells us that this can be done, that we can be released from our psychic prison. We can declare independence from our false-self. This declaration comes next, in Step 3.

> **Step 3:** Made a decision to turn our will and our lives over to the care of God *as we understood Him.*
>
> **Therapeutic Effect:** Making a commitment to a new way of life—to uncover, discover, and honor our true-self.

Hope without affirmative or appropriate action is nothing but an empty promise. We need to make a decision to cut away our dependence on our false-self and seek a new way of being that is based on a power greater than our false-self—that is based on our real-self or higher self or on a God of our understanding.

The false-self was based on a desire for power. We wanted power and control over our lives and the feelings of others. Our false-self was going to lead us down a path that would yield top approval, perfection, security, and an ideal romance. Not once did we consider that this was the problem rather than the solution—until we woke up. We realized in Step 2 that there is hope, but only if we pursue a different course, only if we listen to the part of ourselves that we abandoned long ago.

Making a decision to find our true-self is essential to changing our lives. If we don't make a wholehearted, disciplined, enduring, and unwavering commitment, we won't be able to tolerate the discomfort that comes from growth. We were forewarned about this when we were told "half measures availed us nothing" (*Alcoholics Anonymous* 2001, 59). I discussed the importance of going to any lengths in recovery in *12 Stupid Things That Mess Up Recovery* (Berger 2008).

We have arrived at a crucial moment in our lives. The effectiveness and resilience of our efforts will be determined by the depth and earnestness of our commitment. Our goal is to seek a better direction for our lives that is not driven or influenced by our false-self or our addiction. We seek a path that leads to true autonomy and independence of spirit. Our goal is freedom from our oppressive false-self, from our emotional dependency, and from our addicted-self. Our goal is to recover our lost true-self.

A curious thing happens when we decide to truly commit ourselves to this new way of life. Something shifts at a very deep level. All sorts of things happen to support our decision that none of us would have foreseen. A whole stream of events flows from our decision that points the way and reinforces our decision. We begin to see that letting go doesn't result in total anarchy and chaos. Quite the contrary: we come to realize that there is a force operating in our lives that is much greater than the "Imperial Self" we have relied on. We start to realize that we can trust the process. We relinquish control and begin to discover a power greater than ourselves, whether it be a God of our own understanding or the life force present in all living things. The point is that we cannot continue to rely on our false-self and its misuse of power if things are going to be different.

Now that we have made a decision to construct a new way of life, what is next? As I have explained, each Step prepares us for the life-changing task inherent in the Step that follows. Steps 1–3 gave us a new foundation and source of strength for our lives. *They helped us deconstruct our false-self while giving us the hope that we can be free from the insanity of our addiction and all the rigidity and expectations of our false-self.*

Now we need to continue the recovery of our true-self. The next four Steps use the foundation built by Steps 1–3 to support a fearless and rigorous inventory of ourselves and sharing the results with a confidant. The self-knowledge and insight we acquire from the next four Steps is critical. It allows us to support ourselves when we make amends to those we have harmed and practice self-awareness, self-regulation, and right conduct.

Let's now see what we are asked to do in Step 4 and how this will help us reconstruct a more positive self-concept.

Chapter 4:

Unpacking the
Therapeutic Value
of Steps 4-7

The first three Steps began the construction of a new foundation for a more positive self-concept, a foundation that will support self-realization. In the next four Steps, we will come to a much deeper understanding of ourselves and a more realistic view of ourselves. We will fearlessly face the self that we have become and begin to see the self that we can evolve into: our possible or true-self. These Steps generate a complete restructuring of who we are and what we know about ourselves.

Step 4: Made a searching and fearless moral inventory of ourselves.

Therapeutic Effect: Increases self-awareness.

In Step 3, we made a decision to find a new way of life. Now we are asked to take a specific action that will further the deconstruction of the false-self and start the process of constructing a more positive self-concept. This Step puts us squarely on the road toward freedom from our psychic prison. The thoroughness of the inventory we are asked to do in Step 4 is the first tangible evidence of the depth and sincerity of our commitment.

Understanding ourselves and the patterns of our behavior is at the heart of all psychotherapies. It is through understanding ourselves and how we function in human relations that we increase our awareness of who we are and who we aren't. Awareness creates the possibility of change. Once we become aware of what we are doing, we can make better choices and aim at developing a better attitude toward ourselves and others. Fritz Perls, the founder of Gestalt therapy, explained it like this: "If we cannot understand ourselves, we can never hope to understand what we are doing, we can never hope to solve our problems, we can never learn to live rewarding lives" (1976, 2). If we are going to live rewarding lives, then we need to become aware of what we do that creates problems in our relationship with ourselves and others, and what causes our self-destructive behavior, whether it be drugs, eating, sexually acting out, or gambling.

The goal of the Fourth Step inventory is to create an awareness of what we are doing and how we do it. Bill Wilson indicated that the inventory helps us

> . . . find exactly how, when, and where our natural desires have warped us. We wish to look squarely at the unhappiness this has caused others and ourselves. By discovering what our emotional deformities are, we can move toward their correction. Without a willing and persistent effort to do this, there can be little sobriety and contentment. (*Twelve Steps and Twelve Traditions* 1981, 43)

We need to develop an understanding of the forces within us that drive us to behave as we do. This is at the root of our problems. "It is from our twisted relations with family, friends, and society at large that many of us have suffered the most. . . . The primary fact that we fail to recognize is our total inability to form a true partnership with another human being" (*Twelve Steps and Twelve Traditions* 1981, 53).

What causes our failure to form true partnerships? Bill Wilson thought that it was egomania; I think our difficulties are better understood as a *lack of differentiation or emotional maturity*. This is not to say we aren't egomaniacs; we clearly are. Egomania, however, is a *result* of a lack of differentiation, not the *cause* of it.

Simply stated, *differentiation* refers to the degree to which we can hold on to ourselves in relationships. The lower our level of differentiation, the more immature we are and the more emotionally reactive we will be. The lower our differentiation, the more emotionally dependent we feel, and the more our self-esteem depends on others and how they respond to our needs. The degree to which we control others corresponds to the degree of our differentiation. Our lack of differentiation drives us to manipulate and control others. We insist on compliance with our demands and rules to make us feel loved or OK about ourselves. As I heard mentioned in a meeting, we don't have relationships—we take hostages. We manipulate people, either by establishing power over them, by being people pleasers and submitting to their wills, or by disinvesting or emotionally withdrawing. It's important to note that we are capable of functioning in any of these ways, but our dominant style is determined by the nature of our false-self. Remember, our false-self was the self we thought we had to be to ensure love and acceptance; it was our path to belonging, to having power and control.

Bill Wilson described our behavior in this way:

Either we insist upon dominating the people we know, or we depend upon them far too much. If we lean too heavily on people, they will sooner or later fail us, for they are human, too, and cannot possibly meet our incessant demands. . . . When we habitually try to manipulate others to our own willful desires, they revolt, and resist us heavily. . . . As we redouble our efforts at control, and continue to fail, our suffering becomes acute and constant. (*Twelve Steps and Twelve Traditions* 1981, 53)

As we unravel the Gordian knot that we have tied, we become aware that our basic needs have been distorted by our fears and anxieties. Fear and anxiety drove us away from our true-self toward a fabricated-self. It drove us away from authenticity toward lies, manipulation, and deception. It made us mistakenly believe that there will never be enough of what we need. Anxiety and fear distorted reality. These thoughts and feelings skewed our development and impaired our ability to form true partnerships. *Our false-self altered the relationship we have with our basic needs.*

Our inventory will reveal that underneath all this nonsense, two natural forces exist. They are: (1) our desire for togetherness, to join or please or cooperate; and (2) our desire to be ourselves, to march to our own beat, and to hold on to our individuality. When these two forces are balanced, we are in *integrity.* I use the word *integrity* to refer to wholeness. When we are in integrity, we are respecting both our need for togetherness and our need for individuality. Balancing our need for togetherness with our need for individuality is important to establishing *emotional well-being.*

A healthy relationship or true partnership occurs when we function with integrity and encourage our partner to do the same. Dr. Walter Kempler (1982), my mentor, used to say that a healthy relationship is when you accept from your partner only that which is given with an open hand. Do you understand what he was saying?

He encouraged us to dissuade our partners from compromising their integrity to satisfy our needs—to refuse something that is not done or given wholeheartedly. This is an act of true love. True love is not about sacrifice; it's about keeping our integrity and encouraging our partner to do the same.

When we honor our integrity and encourage our partner to do the same, we have a true partnership based on adult, or mature, love. Mature love is when you consider your partner's feelings and desires to be as important as yours, not less or more important. It's union with the preservation of integrity, as Dr. Erich Fromm (1956) pointed out.

Peace of mind and serenity can only be achieved through a willingness to experience discomfort in order to grow. We need to see how our emotional dependency warped us and damaged our relationships—how it built a psychic prison from which the only escape seemed to be alcohol, other drugs, or other forms of acting out. We need to understand how our emotional dependency fragmented us into many disharmonious parts that filled us with unresolved conflict. We need to admit that we treated others as objects to gratify our needs and to realize that we created disharmony and conflict and pain in our relationships. We need to understand that our relationships were based on treating ourselves and the people we love as objects we could manipulate. Our relationships were "it to it" in their nature, rather than more personal and healthy relationships, which are based on "I to Thou." (I will talk more about the "I to Thou" relationship in Hidden Reward 11.) It's not easy to face our mistakes, especially when we have high expectations for how we are supposed to behave.

Tamerin and Neumann (1974) described us in this way: "In contrast to the stereotype of the alcoholic individual as irresponsible, negligent, disorderly and indifferent, when sober he is usually highly responsible, conscientious, orderly, cautious, and often a perfectionist, placing inordinately high performance demands on himself" (16). These characteristics are symptoms of the false-self, and they make it hard for us to look at ourselves honestly.

Therefore we need to expect that we will feel uncomfortable doing Step 4. It's a very difficult task. My dear friend Herb K. conducts a yearlong workshop on the Twelve Steps. His workshops are very popular. He begins each year with about two hundred participants. Even though he attracts a select group of folks who are highly motivated and serious about recovery, he still has a very high dropout rate. Approximately 75 percent of the participants drop out when he reaches Step 4.

My explanation for this high dropout rate is that these individuals don't want to face the truth about themselves. They are afraid. You've heard the saying that the truth will set you free. The whole truth is that the truth will set you free *if you have the courage to face the truth and integrate it into your life.* This is why the moral inventory needs to be "searching and fearless." It needs to be done fearlessly because we need to see ourselves as we are, and not tainted by our false-self. *Our false-self makes what's right seem wrong, and what's wrong seem right.* We can't respect these false beliefs if we are going to recover.

Our false-self dictated who we should be. Any time we broke its rules, we felt ashamed and hated ourselves. Any trait or characteristic that wasn't acceptable to it became our despised-self. This hated self was a depository for all the parts of us that we had to disown, that we weren't proud of, that weren't acceptable to the false-self. To be rigorously honest with ourselves we cannot let our false-self influence the nature of the inventory. We need to own those things that we have despised or hated about ourselves. This truth seeking about ourselves requires extraordinary courage and boldness to see ourselves as we are. Remember: even though we have made mistakes, we aren't a mistake!

Once we have completed our searching and fearless moral inventory, we are ready to take the next step in the development of a positive self-concept. Solitary self-appraisal is insufficient. We need to reconnect with our humanity and learn how to trust and be vulnerable. We need to surrender our self-reliance and experience the value of an enlightened witness.

> **Step 5:** Admitted to God, to ourselves, and to another human being the exact nature of our wrongs.

> **Therapeutic Effect:** Teaches us the value of an enlightened witness as well as the importance of a relationship based on vulnerability and authenticity.

Step 4 had us conduct a searching and fearless moral inventory. For many of us, this was the first time we had been rigorously honest with ourselves. During this soul-searching process we learned a lot about ourselves and our human relations. We may sum up what we uncovered in this simple way: we were more than we thought we were and less than we thought we were. We discovered that when we set aside the judgment of our false-self and its many "shoulds," it was easier to be honest with ourselves, face our shortcomings, and recognize our assets.

We also came to see that we are living a paradox—that we are simultaneously *being* and *becoming*. This gave us hope that we could restructure our selves, that we could develop our better self and a better attitude toward life. This is something we never would have believed before we started this journey. Our false-self turned the world into a state of absolutes; there was no gray. Either we met the demands of our false-self or we failed completely. Either we are perfect or we are nothing. There was never a sense of ourselves as a work in progress. I am reminded of a bumper sticker I saw on a car in front of me as I was driving south on the 405 Freeway that put a smile on my face. It read: "Please be patient with me, God isn't finished with me yet!"

Insights like these helped us realize that there is much more to life than we saw through the lens created by our addict-self and false-self. A new vision of ourselves and life started to take shape. Step 4 helped us conduct an honest self-appraisal like never before; now we are ready to take the next step in our development.

The Twelve Steps are designed to deconstruct our false-self and promote a sense of humility. We've done a fairly good job of it by the time we arrive at the doorstep of the Fifth Step, but this Step asks us to cross a new threshold—one that we have never dared cross before. We are asked to be open and vulnerable with another person and with a God of our understanding. We are instructed to confide in this person and in the God of our understanding, and to admit the exact nature of our wrongs. When it comes to this, no Step is harder than Step 5.

We are about to rewrite a demand of the false-self, which tells us that the only person we can rely upon is ourselves. It tells us not to air our dirty laundry in public—that someone will use what we share against us. It makes us cynical and distrustful.

To deconstruct our false-self, we have to disobey its rules. In the Twelve Step program, this is referred to as "ego deflation." Step 5 instructs us to share the results of our fearless inventory with another person, an enlightened witness. "Hence it was most evident that a solitary self-appraisal, and the admission of our defects based upon that alone, wouldn't be nearly enough. We'd have to have outside help if we were surely to know and admit the truth about ourselves" (*Twelve Steps and Twelve Traditions* 1981, 59).

We are going to be extremely vulnerable with this person and open our hearts to him or her. We are going to take off our mask and be authentic. This goes against the defiant self-reliance that we developed as a result of our false-self. We were the masters of our own fate; we ran the show. We didn't trust anyone to do it for us. Now we need to take a leap of faith. We need to find someone we can trust for this fearless admission. We needed to find an enlightened witness.

An enlightened witness is someone who can listen to us with an open mind and a compassionate heart. Someone who won't be judgmental, but will rather see our true essence. Someone who will look beyond our behavior and see the positive intention in our struggles. An enlightened witness is someone who has done their own work, faced their own demons, and turned their weakness into a strength. This may be a sponsor from our Twelve Step program, a therapist we have been working with, or a member of the clergy.

Our relationship with an enlightened witness will help us move toward self-acceptance and humility. Step 5 creates a new kinship with our fellows. It helps us see that we are not alone: the issues we struggle with are universal. We are human *beings* who share many similarities with our fellows.

Those of us who struggle with addiction will also realize that many of the hurtful things we did to others were best understood as symptoms of our addiction. Addiction hijacked our brain and impaired our judgment. What was wrong seemed right. While we are not to blame for our addiction, we are responsible for our recovery and for the damage we have inflicted on ourselves and others.

We will never achieve serenity and peace of mind if we don't accept responsibility for our actions and clean house, if we don't learn to turn to others for help, and if we don't learn from our mistakes.

We need to move toward an authentic relationship with

ourselves, with our higher power, and with others. The Fifth Step teaches us the value of authenticity and the importance of having an enlightened witness in our lives. These two factors will be essential in our recovery.

Now that we have opened ourselves up and faced ourselves courageously and truthfully, we are ready for the next task that will help us recover our lost true-self. We are ready to build upon the knowledge we have gained by being honest with ourselves and someone else. We are ready to aim at becoming our best possible self and to develop even more insight into our shortcomings.

Step 6: Were entirely ready to have God remove all these defects of character.

Therapeutic Effect: Aiming at becoming our best self.

The ability to step up and accept the responsibility to change our defects of character separates the willing from the unwilling. Our commitment to rid ourselves of those character flaws that caused problems with our fellows and with society at large is at the heart of the spirit of recovery. We are aiming at becoming our best self. We must remember, however, that desire doesn't equal ability.

It is unreasonable for us to expect to rise above all our character defects and ascend into the hallowed halls of saints. We cannot; it's impossible. Instead of expecting the impossible, we will have to be content with steady improvement. Striving for progress rather than perfection is the best attitude we can take toward becoming our best possible self.

Our inventory and fearless admission of the nature of our wrongs helped us identify our false-self and all its shortcomings. We now have a good idea of who we are and who we aren't. Step 6 helps us understand character defects from a totally different perspective;

we are now going to understand their purpose in our lives. This Step helps us realize that there are forces operating within us that might resist change. We need to understand these forces if we are going to be able to remove our character defects. Our goal here is to continue to untangle the roots of our false-self that have so insidiously wrapped themselves around the roots of our real-self. This will take time and patience, but if we endure we will develop a new understanding of ourselves, and more will be revealed about our true nature. Much more.

Dr. James Bugental, an existential humanistic therapist, defined resistance as "the impulse to protect one's familiar identity and known world against a perceived threat" (1987, 175). Our fabricated-self forms the basis for our identity and our worldview. This is who we believe we are. It is what is familiar to us, while the true-self is not. The true-self is a stranger, an alien. The true-self is like an acorn that has never grown into the oak tree. We therefore are much more familiar with our false-self than we are with our true-self. The strength of the resistance we will run into will be proportionate to the degree that we have identified with our false-self. The more we identified with our false-self, the more resistance we will experience in letting it go.

Let me give you an example from a clinical experience. I had a very powerful session with a man who was attending one of my retreats on emotional sobriety. Fifty-three men had gathered with me at a beautiful retreat center near Wappinger Falls, New York, to explore their emotional recovery. In these retreats, I use Bill Wilson's 1958 *Grapevine* article on emotional sobriety to discuss the issues within us that interfere with our emotional sobriety (Wilson 1988c).

Bill Wilson identified his "almost absolute dependence" on people, places, and things for his emotional well-being as his problem (1988c, 237). His self-esteem depended on how people reacted to him. It was dependent on things going according to his expectations. I refer to this as *emotional dependency*. Emotional dependency causes serious problems in our human relations. It generates a set of rules that specify how our partner needs to behave in order for us to feel loved and accepted. We try to regulate others to meet our expectations so that we feel OK. Our emotional dependency creates unenforceable rules. When we are upset, it is because someone is not adhering to our demands.

One of the men at the retreat, we will call him Roberto, discussed how upset he was with his wife and son. I asked him to be more specific. He said that when either one of them did the dishes, they left them sitting in the drying rack in the sink instead of drying them off and putting them away, which is how the dishes should be done. It infuriated him that they ignored his wishes. When I told him that he was being unreasonable, he became indignant. "You got to be kidding me, Doc!" He explained that "they weren't doing things the way they were supposed to do them."

What he didn't realize is that his unrelenting demands were based on an unhealthy dependency that made him take their behavior personally. That is the belief that hooked him. If his wife and son complied, it would make him feel accepted and validated. He would feel loved. Their lack of cooperation meant that he was insignificant. The reflected sense of himself that he saw in their disobedience made him feel rejected, hurt, and angry. His unenforceable rule was: "You must do things the way I want you to because it will make me feel loved and accepted." His false-self demanded obedience. He raged at them when he didn't get it, trying to intimidate them into compliance. They weren't caving in, and he didn't know what to do. He was in a panic, desperate for their love, which made him even more demanding and tyrannical.

I confronted him about his rules, but this wasn't getting him any closer to seeing what he was doing. Remember, we have a way of making the unreasonable seem reasonable. He couldn't see what he was doing; he was too invested in his way of being. Then it hit me: I wondered who in his past had taught him that "doing things the way they were supposed to do them" was the most important rule in life. I asked him if he could remember a time in his life when someone made following outside rules more important than understanding him, his feelings, his aspirations—his *life*. He paused, and then put his head into his hands. He started crying.

When I asked him what was going on, he said that he felt embarrassed. I tried to make it OK that he was crying by telling him that he must have remembered something very painful because his pain broke through his defenses. He went on to tell me that his childhood was very sterile (my word, not his). His mother spent more time ironing his underwear than she spent enjoying time with him. His father was never home because he worked all the time; he picked coffee beans and worked late into the night and on weekends. Roberto was emotionally neglected as a child, which left a large hole in his heart. His mother and father justified their method of childrearing. This is the way things had to be, they told him. What happened next started his emotional recovery.

I told him that the pain he was experiencing was the same pain that his wife and child felt when he made the dishes more important than them. Wow, what an insight! His eyes opened wide, and he cried even harder. He had broken the trance that his false-self had placed on him. He could now see the reality and real effects of his behavior. He was now ready to let go of this character defect: making things more important than people.

Dr. Kempler (1982), my mentor of more than twenty years, taught me that shortcomings or character defects serve several different purposes in our lives. They do three things: (1) they economize our emotional distress; (2) they are a cry for help; and (3) they communicate the experience we need to resolve it.

Do you see how this applies to Roberto? By identifying with his parents' way of doing things, he economized his distress. He made what was wrong and painful to him, right. He justified making things more important than people. This was the way the world was supposed to work.

This was also his cry for help. He was distressed by constantly being at odds with his wife and son. The conflict alienated him from their love. He missed them. The fact that he had made things more important than people also told me that he needed to learn how to make people more important than things.

In preparation to rid ourselves of our character defects, it is important to understand that they served a purpose. "What we must recognize now is that we exult in some of our defects. We really love them. Who, for example, doesn't like to feel just a little superior to the next fellow, or even quite a lot superior? Isn't it true that we like to let greed masquerade as ambition?" (*Twelve Steps and Twelve Traditions* 1981, 66). When we understand the purpose of our defects, we can get on with the business of replacing them with authenticity and more effective ways of dealing with our needs.

Getting honest with ourselves and working through our resistance to remove some of our character defects are important parts of the change process. We are preparing to rid ourselves of the defects promoted by our false-self. We are preparing ourselves to take responsibility for who we are and who we aren't. We are preparing to restructure our self.

When responsibility is fused with blame, it creates a block that interferes with mobilizing and motivating ourselves to change. When blame is fused with responsibility, we will marshal our defenses and avoid facing who we really are and what we have done (Amodeo

1994). Responsibility is self-empowering and is not to be confused with blame, which is paralyzing. We are not taking responsibility if we blame ourselves for what we have done wrong. This is how our false-self fools us into thinking we are doing something about a problem when we aren't. These are futile self-improvement games. Blaming ourselves is a part of the problem, not a part of the solution.

Responsibility empowers us and facilitates the positive restructuring of our self-concept. It motivates us to strive toward being the best possible version of ourselves. Step 6 helps us see the function of our character defects to prepare us to let go of them. We can't fix these shortcomings alone. We need each other and the help of our higher power. We need to put the best in us in charge of the worst in us.

Asking for help in dealing with our character defects is what we are going to do next, in Step 7.

Step 7: Humbly asked Him to remove our shortcomings.

Therapeutic Effect: Develops humility and the ability to ask for help in restructuring ourselves.

There are different kinds of humility. Early on in recovery, humility was the result of "a forced feeding on humble pie" (*Twelve Steps and Twelve Traditions* 1981, 74). We had to be beaten into submission and surrender by our addiction. This experience helped us understand that self-reliance wasn't the answer to our problems, contrary to what our false-self led us to believe. Instead, we eventually realized that our defiant self-reliance was at the heart of our problem. As our reliance on a power greater than our false-self increased, we found immense personal value in this new allegiance. We began to view humility as our ally, something that would nourish a positive self-concept and help us change old and outdated ideas. One specific idea that had to change was our attitude toward pain and discomfort.

Our false-self told us that the goal of life was to feel comfortable, to feel in control, to be free of anxiety, and to be happy. It told us that life should be easy. This philosophy encouraged us to avoid painful experiences or emotional discomfort. We became obsessed with feeling good and would do anything or use anything to achieve this state of mind. We became masters in the art of avoidance and manipulation. We were like Houdini: we found a way to escape any difficult situation. Because we avoided discomfort, we never learned to manage our anxiety or soothe our pain or lick our wounds. We never learned to regulate and modulate our feelings. Our immaturity forced us to rely on drugs and manipulation to manage our feelings.

Avoidance stunted our growth and development. There is no easier, softer way to grow up than to suffer and learn from pain. Fritz Perls, the father of Gestalt therapy, didn't pull any punches when he confronted us about this issue. He stated, "We are phobic, we avoid suffering, especially the suffering of frustration. We are spoiled and don't want to go through the hellgates of suffering. We stay immature, we go on manipulating the world, rather than to suffer the pains of growing up" (1969, 56).

So what does it mean that our path to maturity must "go through the hellgates of suffering"? It means that we have to be willing to face what we have done wrong and those whom we have hurt. It means we have to be willing to experience frustration or sadness or pain or uncertainty, and that we may have to look foolish to stop acting foolishly.

Fully experiencing and being present to our feelings is a new way of being for us. We must endure our pain or frustration because we need to in order to restore our true-self. We begin to see that facing our anxiety, and sitting with discomfort, leads to growth. We realize that the more discomfort we are willing to tolerate, the more peace of mind and serenity we will eventually enjoy.

In this Step we are beginning to see that our desire to grow, to be self-actualized, is a very different kind of motivation. This motivation, based on a desire to grow, provides a solid foundation for our recovery. It is not temporary and short-lived like a motivation based on fixing a problem. Deficit-based motivation only lasts as long as there is a problem. We need something more robust than this if we are going to endure the struggles we will face in recovery.

Accepting our limitations and asking for help when we need it are important if we are going to become fully functioning human beings. A fully functioning person welcomes help and can allow himself or herself to be influenced without feeling diminished or ashamed. A fully functioning person can ask for help to change destructive and harmful behaviors. Attaining humility is necessary to the restructuring of our self-concept. Without humility, it becomes impossible to embrace the tasks set before us in Steps 8–10.

Because of the work we have done in the previous Steps, we have come to realize that our values are all screwed up, that we lost sight of what was truly important. Bill Wilson stated it this way: "We had lacked the perspective to see that character-building and spiritual values had to come first, and that material satisfactions were not the purpose of living" (*Twelve Steps and Twelve Traditions* 1981, 71). We learned that we had to shift our consciousness from a life based on having (materialism) to one based on being (spirituality). We shifted our focus to who we are rather than what we had.

When we shift our emotional center of gravity to within ourselves, we no longer focus on the outcome of our actions for validation. We realize that doing the right thing is intrinsically rewarding. We shift our emotional security from an other-validated self-esteem to a self-validated self-esteem. We are going to need to hold on to this perspective to support us in the work that lies ahead.

Steps 1–7 have restructured our relationship with ourselves. We let go of our reliance on our false-self and have, in earnest, begun replacing it with a higher self, a true-self. We are aiming at becoming our best self, and to do that we have to step up and accept responsibility to change.

In Steps 8 and 9, we are going to shift our focus from self to others. We are going to focus on improving our relationships with others. First we will see how our false-self has harmed our relationships, and then we will go about the business of repairing them.

Steps 8, 9, and 10 form the basis for our emotional well-being. They are concerned with our emotional recovery. Let's now turn to a comprehensive discussion of these Steps. Remember, Step 7 set us up for Step 8. We asked for help to remove our shortcomings, and now we are guided to take a very specific action to help us rid ourselves of our character defects, an action that will help us develop the best possible attitude we can take toward human relations.

Chapter 5:
Making Amends:
Working Steps 8, 9, and 10

Working the first seven Steps helped us develop a new, more positive and realistic relationship with ourselves. We are more in harmony with ourselves now. The civil war that raged within has started to quiet down. We are also more realistic about who we are and who we are not. We have discovered and connected to a power greater than our false-self: a higher power. We have experienced a major shift in our attitude toward ourselves and life. As Chuck C., a famous author who wrote about the lessons he learned in recovery, claimed, it is like we have put on a new pair of glasses. We are relating to ourselves in a new, much healthier way. We had to change. Our old ways weren't working.

We tried to be someone we weren't. We tried to live up to a set of impossible standards established by a fabricated-self, and when we did we felt a sense of pride, which is quite unfortunate. This is not real pride. It is a false-pride, based on living up to the standards set by the false-self.

Our false-pride caused many of our woes. It interfered with our ability to be present and flow with our experiences. It made it impossible to learn from our experience and prevented us from taking responsibility and making amends when we were wrong or hurt others. We always had to win or be right. Our false-pride crippled our maturity and delayed our growth. How can we thrive when we are driven by false-pride to be the self we are not?

We are beginning to relate to ourselves better, now that we are more grounded in reality and self-acceptance. We can think about what happened in Steps 1–7 by considering the direction of the change that has taken place in our lives. Change involves movement away from certain negative attitudes and behaviors, and movement toward more fulfilling attitudes and behaviors.

Away from the Self That We Are Not, and toward the Self That We Are

We've realized a very important fact: until we let go of the beliefs rooted in our false-self, our efforts to change will be futile. Hitting bottom helped us surrender the absurd idea that we didn't need help and that we should be ashamed to accept it. We are moving away from the belief that we alone can provide the answers to our problems and that we should be an island of self-sufficiency. We are moving away from playing games or playing God and needing to control everything and everyone. We are moving away from our instinct to run away when things become difficult or we feel uncomfortable. We are moving away from needing to be perfect to be OK, and believing that we need to be the self that we are not.

We are moving toward a relationship with ourselves that is grounded in who we really are: our real-self. We are moving toward letting go of the need to control, and toward keeping in close contact with our experience. We are moving toward having faith in our basic need to grow and become whole, and toward taking total responsibility for who we have become and what we have done, including taking responsibility for the harm we have caused ourselves and others.

The work we have done in Steps 1–7 has set us firmly on the road to self-acceptance and has broken the trance induced by our culture and our false-self. We now see that our false-self was the problem, not the solution. We have found a power greater than ourselves that has helped us achieve a new self-understanding. But our work is far from over.

Steps 1–7 gave us a better relationship with ourselves. Now we need to shift our focus to developing better relationships with our fellows.

Steps 8, 9, and 10 Are the Keys to Healthier Human Relations and Emotional Well-Being

We cannot have healthier relationships without a persistent effort to keep our side of the street clean. A sincere effort at righting our wrongs begins our emotional recovery. These three Steps help us apply what we have learned about who we are and who we aren't, so that we can have better relationships. This is what Earnie Larsen (1985), an expert on the process of recovery, called *Stage II recovery*. Stage II recovery is concerned with learning how to have healthier relationships. It's concerned with the quality of our connections. To have healthier relationships, we need to take responsibility for our self-esteem, because without self-esteem, we will never feel worthy of happiness, success, or love.

When we step up and take on these tasks, we will begin to know emotional well-being—but only if we are willing to experience discomfort in order to grow. There is no pain-free, easier, or softer way. We are going to need to face our mistakes and keep a solid alliance with ourselves as we sail into these uncharted waters. There are many dangerous currents (such as false-pride) and riptides (such as self-hate) that lie ahead, and if we don't support ourselves on this journey we will end up failing. We will end up sinking, drowning, or even relapsing.

Our efforts in working Steps 8, 9, and 10 provide tangible evidence of our sincerity and the depth of our commitment to this new way of life. As you will soon see, making amends and promptly admitting we are wrong gives us twelve hidden rewards that no one could have imagined would come their way at the beginning of this journey.

Working Step 8

Step 8: Made a list of all persons we had harmed, and became willing to make amends to them all.

Therapeutic Effect: Being accountable for our actions increases our trustworthiness and self-esteem.

These instructions seem simple and straightforward, don't they? We are asked to make a list of everyone we have harmed and become willing to make amends to all of them. Although these instructions seem simple, following them is not very easy or straightforward.

Here's what makes this Step so challenging: we are being asked to break a basic rule of our false-self, which once demanded that we had to be perfect, that we had to be superhuman to be OK. Being human wasn't enough; we had to become someone we were not. We had to be more than human. We rejected ourselves to become a fabricated-self. We became phonies, living behind a fabricated facade.

By listing everyone we have harmed, we are facing our faults.

We are tearing down our facade and facing our humanity. We are dispelling the myth of perfection that the false-self created. We are being accountable, honest, and humble. We are not running or hiding from the truth; we are facing ourselves, as we are, and becoming willing to correct our mistakes. *Only the best in us can face the worst in us.* We need the best in us to take the lead.

Dr. Nathaniel Branden (1994), one of the foremost authorities on self-esteem, identified six characteristics that people with high self-esteem possess. Taking responsibility was number one. Branden found that individuals with high self-esteem accept total responsibility for the quality of their lives. This doesn't mean that they are self-reliant; they aren't. It means that they take responsibility to ask for help when they need it, and they admit when they are wrong and learn from those actions. Steps 8, 9, and 10 are consistent with Dr. Branden's lessons about individuals with high self-esteem. When we follow these three Steps, we are learning how to have *real* self-esteem. This is why we must go to great lengths to generate a comprehensive list of all persons we have harmed. This is the path toward emotional freedom and a solid sense of self.

The list we create needs to be inclusive rather than selective or exclusive. This is important because we can't trust our false-pride. It will rationalize some of our inappropriate behaviors as justified or reasonable or conclude that we shouldn't include a certain person on our list for one reason or another. After all, weren't *we* the injured party? Weren't *we* the ones who were betrayed or hurt? Weren't we simply taking an "eye for an eye"? This sort of thinking is destructive to the task at hand.

Remember, there is a part of us that has a way of making what's wrong seem right. So we can't leave any stone unturned. We don't want to deprive ourselves and others of this opportunity to find true peace of mind. Our list must be based on reality, on what we have done to others that harmed them, regardless of what they have done to us. We are making a list of who *we* have harmed, not a list of who has harmed *us*.

In this Step, we are focused on taking responsibility for our transgressions without focusing on the behavior of others. This doesn't mean that we too weren't the victims of someone's selfish or cruel behavior. We probably were. This is unfortunately a part of life, and important to address too, but not at this time. Here we are focused on what we have done wrong. But there is an interesting benefit from working this Step: as we seek forgiveness, we will become more forgiving.

Immediately we see some of the benefits of Step 8. We are learning about forgiveness, what it takes to develop self-esteem, and how to stand on our own two feet. We are recovering our integrity, while letting the best in us take charge. We are holding ourselves accountable to our own ethical and moral standards because it is the right thing to do, not because we expect others to reciprocate or because we'll get a pat on the back or a place in heaven. We are learning to do the right thing because it is the right thing to do and because it is intrinsically rewarding. We are moving away from our need for external validation and becoming self-supportive. We are learning to validate ourselves. We are moving toward forgiving ourselves and others. We are moving to a place beyond right and wrong where we take responsibility for ourselves and our actions.

Up to now we have lived in a tit-for-tat world, and we responded in kind because we did not have a solid sense of self. We had a highly reactive self. We made other people and their limited perceptions of us too important. We wanted love, acceptance, or power at any cost. By shifting our emotional center of gravity to others, our emotional well-being became dependent on them. We used their reactions to us to determine how we should feel about ourselves. This demonstrates a "reflected sense of self," an idea discussed by Dr. David Schnarch, an outstanding sex and marital therapist (1997). This sense of self created the need for other-validated self-esteem, which made us highly reactive. It lowered the threshold of our reactions, because everything that happened to us had implications for our self-esteem. We took things personally—way too personally.

It's noteworthy that taking things too personally is one of the three things that happen when a grievance is formed. Dr. Fred Luskin, a Stanford health psychologist and cofounder and director of the Stanford University Forgiveness Project, reasoned that to facilitate forgiveness one first needs to understand the psychological process that creates a grievance. "To form a grievance that interfered with your life," he says, "you have done the following three things: (1) took the offense too personally, (2) blamed the offender for how you feel, and (3) created a grievance story" (2002, 13).

Dr. Luskin's insights are important for us and our work. These insights will help us make restitution and restorative amends. Understanding the effects of our behavior on those we have harmed will help us address all the issues we need to address when making our amends. It will also help us forgive others.

Making a List of All Those We Have Harmed and Learning from It

I want to give you a few suggestions to help generate a list of the people you have harmed. These suggestions will help you make amends. In the appendix you will find a form to assist you with Step 8.

In the first column, identify the person you have harmed. Write his or her name and the type of relationship the two of you had. In the second column, describe in detail what happened and what you did that hurt this person. Be as specific as you can. This will help you and your sponsor or therapist determine the kind of damage you did or harm you caused the person.

In the third column, note the kind of damage or harm you have done to this person. We have harmed people in many different ways with our insatiable need for power and control. Some of us have been physically and verbally abusive or neglectful. Some of us have raped, molested, or tortured someone, or even taken loved ones hostage. We have unmercifully manipulated family and friends to bend to our desires. We were relentless in demanding our way. We embezzled money to support our addiction or used money that our family needed for rent or food to support our habits. We betrayed the trust of everyone close to us and took advantage of work relationships to cover our tracks. We controlled others with our emotional tirades, our anxiety, or our depression. We wrestled with others to get what we thought we needed without caring about what we were doing to them. Your own actions or attitudes may have hurt people in more than one way. List them all.

In the last column, write out the amends that you need to make. It's essential that you are honest with yourself here; if you are insincere in making amends, don't bother. Your insincerity will do more harm than good.

Let me give you an example of how one of my clients filled out this inventory. Jennifer was forty years old when she celebrated one year of sobriety. She had been married for twenty years to Phil, who was fifty years old. They had two daughters, Karlie and Katie, who were seventeen and fifteen years old, respectively.

Jennifer's alcoholic drinking had started ten years earlier, when she was thirty years old and her children were seven and five. Her husband, who was the love of her life, was beside himself after her drinking took a turn for the worse. He implored her to stop drinking, telling her that she just needed to find something else to do with her life. "Maybe you are bored and need a hobby," he'd say. At other times, he'd tell her to stop hanging around with Carmen, whose heavy drinking was a bad influence. Phil was well intentioned, but naive. Jennifer needed help, not recreational therapy or a change of friends.

Jennifer would often drink and drive. She promised herself that she wouldn't drink and drive with her daughters in the car, as if this made it OK to drink and drive. Remember, alcoholics and addicts are masters at making something wrong seem right. For about six months, she honored this promise. However, as her alcoholism progressed she rationalized breaking the promise because she didn't want to continue to be a burden to her friends by asking them to drive. In reality it had nothing to do with being a burden to her friends. She was embarrassed that she was drinking daily and didn't want anyone to see how bad her drinking had become. So she broke her promise and endangered her girls. Phil suspected that she was drinking and driving, but chose to ignore the problem.

One Thursday afternoon, Jennifer was driving Karlie and Katie to dance practice when she was pulled over by the police. She failed the field sobriety test and was immediately arrested. The Department of Children and Family Services was contacted, and the girls were taken into protective custody in separate homes. When Phil was informed that his wife had been arrested and his girls were being held in protective custody, he asked if they could be released to his custody. His request was denied because he had failed to protect the girls from their mother's alcoholism. What a blessing this turned out to be for Jennifer's family! The crisis that eventually forced them to get help could have been much worse, as you can imagine.

Jennifer surrendered and went into a ninety-day treatment program, where Phil and the girls joined her for family week. They were beginning recovery together, as a family. But instead of being grateful for her family's support, she felt unworthy. Jennifer was filled with shame and humiliation. How could any decent mother do this to her family? She hated herself for the harm she had caused her husband and her daughters. Let's look at how Jennifer filled out the inventory for the harm she had caused her youngest daughter, Katie.

In the first column, she put Katie's name and specified that she was Katie's mother. In the second column, which concerns what happened, she described how she would drink and drive with Katie in the car. She specifically discussed the time that she was arrested and Katie was taken into protective custody. She went into great detail in order to be as honest with herself as she could about what really happened. This should not be the watered-down version. You need to describe the cruel, hard facts in the second column. Being specific will help determine the harm that was caused.

In the third column, Jennifer had to describe the kind of harm she had caused Katie with her behavior. She stated that she had betrayed Katie's trust and failed her motherly duties. She acknowledged that her behavior made Katie feel unsafe and unprotected. She owned that she had physically endangered Katie by driving drunk and took responsibility that her negligent behavior resulted in Katie being taken into protective custody. Katie remained in custody for three weeks before she was reunited with her father and sister. Jennifer talked about how this had traumatized Katie and caused her a tremendous amount of anxiety. She also recognized how she had embarrassed and humiliated Katie at school. Three of Katie's friends' parents found out about Jennifer's arrest and forbade their daughters to play with Katie.

Jennifer sobbed as she wrote out the harm she had caused her daughter. This is not the kind of mother she wanted to be. She needed to face this pain head-on if she was ever going to forgive herself. In the last column, Jennifer wrote out her amends to Katie. Here is what she wrote:

My Dearest Katie,

I failed you terribly. I betrayed your trust; I failed to protect you from my alcoholism and my irresponsible decisions. My negligence caused you to be taken away from your home and put in custody with strangers. I endangered you physically. I tore apart your world and traumatized you. I am terribly sorry for embarrassing you at school and with your friends. I refused to face my problem with alcohol and made you pay a terrible price because of it. I made you feel like you had to take care of me, rather than me taking care of you. I stole your childhood from you, your joy, and emotionally and spiritually wounded you.

When you are ready to let me know how you feel about these terrible things I have done I promise to listen with an open heart and mind. You are not responsible to protect me from your feelings or from what I have done to harm you and our family. I am responsible for what I have done to you and to try and make things better. I want to be there for you now—in whatever way you need me to. If there are some things I have forgotten to make amends for please let me know. I am terribly sorry for hurting you.

I trust that you can imagine what a powerful encounter this was when she made her amends to her daughter. She asked for my support and asked Katie to join her in a session. She read her amends to Katie, and it opened up a very authentic and healing discussion that left us all in tears.

You Know What You Did Wrong!

I don't need to tell you what you have done wrong or how you have been hurtful. You already know! It's just that you don't want other people to know that you know, because then they might be even more upset with you, since you haven't done anything to make amends or clean up your act. This is the difficult truth that we need to face: our avoidance has made things worse. Much worse. We have made our false-pride more important than integrity. We have made winning more important than connecting, and we have made being right more important than being real. Our priorities are out of sync with our best self.

Although it is important to recognize that our avoidance has made things worse, I don't want you to beat yourself up with it. Instead I want you to motivate yourself to stop running away. There is no time better than right now to make things right.

The selfish, self-centered, and cruel choices we have made have left a tremendous amount of pain and suffering in their wake. This is the unfortunate result of what happens when "instincts collide." This is what happens when we view the world and the people in our lives as objects. It's hard to admit that the only value we saw in a person was based on what that person could or couldn't do for us. But that's how we were.

By examining our list, we can see a pattern in our destructive behavior. In *Twelve Steps and Twelve Traditions,* Bill Wilson described the process in the following way:

> While the purpose of making restitution to others is paramount, it is equally necessary that we extricate from an examination of our personal relations every bit of information about ourselves and our fundamental difficulties that we can. Since defective relations with

other human beings have nearly always been the immediate cause of our woes, including our alcoholism, no field of investigation could yield more satisfying and valuable rewards than this one. (1981, 80)

So what are you learning about yourself? Are you beginning to see how unreasonable you are? Can you see how you have objectified others and used them to satisfy your needs without caring about the effect that this would have on them? Do you see your cruelty, or your sadistic side? Can you see how you have avoided stepping up and facing your mistakes? Do you see that there was a part of you that knew what you were doing was wrong, but you did it anyway? Are you seeing how manipulative you were, how emotionally dependent you are, and how your dependency makes you reactive? These are important questions for you to answer.

On Becoming Willing

What can we do to become willing to take on such a humiliating task as facing those we have hurt? How do we motivate ourselves to take on such an onerous task? Praying for willingness is always a good option. But we can also remind ourselves that we are aiming for the best possible relationship with our fellows. This requires that we become trustworthy, something we haven't been.

If we aren't willing to own up to our mistakes or take responsibility when we do something wrong, we will never be trustworthy. Instead of taking responsibility for our harmful behavior, for abusing and lying to others, we twisted things around. We tried to make our victims believe that it was their fault that we abused them or lied to them. We covered up our mistakes with justifications, rationalizations, and excuses. When we did recognize the needs or feelings of others, it was to manipulate them into giving us another chance. We really didn't care about their feelings, or we would have changed our behavior. We were phonies and manipulative. This is a tough thing to face about ourselves, and yet it is vital to restoring the trust we have broken.

If we are going to recover the trust that we have lost, we need to make amends to those we have hurt. We can only restore the trust we shattered by humbling ourselves, being willing to make restitution to those we have hurt, and being willing to go to any lengths to restore their wholeness.

It Is Important That We Support Ourselves and Get Support

The last thing I want to say to you about working this Step is don't do it alone, and you don't have to. The importance of having an enlightened witness oversee this task cannot be overstated. We need help because it is very easy to fall out of one side of the bed or the other; we can either minimize our actions or exaggerate them. I don't want you to understate the damage you have done to others, nor do I want you to overstate what you have done. Having help can allow us to be more objective. We need help in sorting out real culpability from taking responsibility for the things we are not responsible for. We may not be very good at discerning the difference. Our pain may distort reality.

Here's an example from Susanna, a young lady I was seeing in therapy who inappropriately felt responsible for the death of a male friend. About four years ago, she was attending the Burning Man gathering in Nevada. Before she left for the event, she got into a terrible fight with her boyfriend and broke up with him. Their relationship had been on shaky ground for some time. Jason was a violent young man who dealt drugs and would often physically or verbally abuse her. He was a member of a very dangerous gang.

After she drove to Burning Man alone, she felt sad and wanted to hang out with someone she knew. So she decided to invite Nick, a previous boyfriend, to join her. She had remained good friends with him after their relationship ended five years previously, which made Jason very jealous. Nick was someone Susanna cared about, but she considered him more of a friend than a love interest.

Jason got wind of what was happening, and while Nick was driving up to Burning Man, Jason ran him off the road. Nick died in the accident, and Jason was convicted of first-degree manslaughter. Regardless of Jason's conviction for this crime, Susanna blamed herself for the death of her friend. She took responsibility for something that was not her fault. She didn't kill Nick; Jason killed him. But she felt guilty. She blamed herself and felt as if she had to make amends to Nick's family. In truth, she was not responsible for what happened to her friend. Jason was.

Guilt may at times be a result of unexpressed pain and resentment. Susanna had a lot of anger at Jason and pain over the loss of Nick that needed to be addressed. This is the path we followed to help her sort out what she was responsible for. Today she knows that it was not her fault that her friend was killed. She is still very sad that this terrible thing happened, but she no longer blames herself or feels that she needs to make amends to his family.

As I mentioned earlier, making a list of the people we have harmed is a difficult task. If you are thorough in making the list and rigorously honest about what you did, then the best in you is in charge. It's a paradox that facing the worst in us can bring out the best in us. But by now we are quite familiar with the power of paradox. Remember the paradoxical theory of change: we change when we own who we are rather than try to be someone we are not.

Step 8 has prepared us for the next step toward emotional recovery and healthy human relations. Now we need to take thoughtful action and, when appropriate, make amends to those we have hurt. That is what Step 9 is all about.

Working Step 9

Step 9: Made direct amends to such people wherever possible, except when to do so would injure them or others.

Therapeutic Effect: Resolving unfinished business and restoring social justice.

Step 8 has helped us identify *who* we need to make amends to, and *what* we need to make amends for. Step 9 is about *how* we are going to go about making amends. Foremost, our attitude needs to be *do no more harm.* This means that we need to be aware of the potential pain we may cause by tearing the scab off someone else's old wound. As Bill Wilson stated, "We must be sure to remember that we cannot buy our own peace of mind at the expense of others" (*Twelve Steps and Twelve Traditions* 1981, 84). This Step is teaching us that mutual respect is an important characteristic of a healthy relationship. We are learning to treat others as though they were as important as we are—no more and no less.

This is a new attitude for us. We used to treat others like they were objects to be manipulated and controlled. We didn't respect them; we maneuvered them to get validation, admiration, acceptance, or love. We were an "it" relating to another "it." We objectified ourselves and others. We weren't personal or intimate in our relationships. We couldn't be, because then we'd find it too difficult to treat someone so poorly.

Step 9 is teaching us that we need to be personal in our relationships if we are going to restore our trustworthiness. Instead of our relationships being based on an "it to it" dynamic, we have to learn how to relate more personally from an "I to Thou" attitude. We have to be more personal if we are going to amend the damage we have done. To restore trust, we have to own our past untrustworthiness.

We have to take responsibility for being manipulative, sadistic, inauthentic, and disingenuous. *Only the best in us can take responsibility for the worst in us.*

We are warned not to begin the process of making amends until the foundation of our recovery is solid. I think this is good advice in most cases, but sometimes making amends will help a chronic relapser develop a more stable recovery.

Cedric had been sober for three years, but then relapsed. For the next five years, he was sober only intermittently. He just couldn't seem to put together any real clean time. Finally he completed a thirty-day inpatient program, after which he was referred to me. He worked hard in therapy and for the most part was doing the right things to stay sober. He had a sponsor, talked with him daily, attended five to seven meetings per week, and helped others. Despite his best efforts he had relapsed twice after several months of sobriety and therapy.

We sat down to put our heads together after his second relapse to see if we could figure out what was missing in his program. As we talked, I had the hunch to ask him about making amends. He took a couple of moments before he responded and said, "I made some amends during the three years I was clean and sober, but I didn't make all of them." Could this be what he needed to do to stabilize his recovery? It was worth a try. I asked him if he was willing to make a list of those he had harmed and set out on a course of making amends to them all when appropriate.

He liked the idea and went after this task as if his life depended on it, because in reality it did. He set out to make amends at least once per day until everyone on his list was checked off. He went to previous employers and made amends for drinking on the job instead of doing what he was paid to do. He sought out ex-girlfriends and made amends for treating them poorly. He sat with his mother and made amends for betraying her trust in him and for manipulating her to get money. He made amends to his two daughters for hurting them. He offered to make restitution to each person he had harmed and asked what he could do to repair the damage he had done. He humbled himself and threw himself at their mercy.

A remarkable thing happened as he righted these wrongs: he became increasingly at peace with himself. A serenity came over him that I had never seen in him before. It's been more than a year now since his last relapse. He continues to work a strong program, taking it one day at a time.

When to Make Amends and When Not to Make Amends

Here are some general guidelines we need to follow:

If making amends to someone will cause more harm than good, we have to make partial amends instead of direct amends.

For instance, Dan and a coworker embezzled money from their company, and they were never discovered. There was a very good chance that if he made amends to his former employer, it would expose his friend as well. Dan did not have a right to seek his own peace of mind at his friend's expense. In this case, he made amends by setting up a schedule to make regular donations to several of the charities his former employer supported until he paid back all the money he had embezzled.

Amends need to be postponed if making them will cause more harm than good.

Mary had betrayed her friend Louise by gossiping about something that Louise had shared with her in confidence. This shattered Louise. What she had shared with Mary was very personal, and she didn't want it to be public knowledge. Mary shared what Louise had disclosed to her with a group of women that they often walked with. It humiliated and embarrassed Louise so much that she quit walking with the group. She withdrew and became a recluse. When Mary was ready to make amends, Louise was not in a good place: her mother had just died suddenly, and Louise was overcome with grief and shock. The stress of revisiting the betrayal she felt from Mary would have caused Louise more harm than good. Mary's sponsor told her to wait a couple of months until it seemed that making her amends would not cause more harm than good.

Bill Wilson reminds us that "it does not lighten our burden when we recklessly make the crosses of others heavier" (*Twelve Steps and Twelve Traditions* 1981, 86). Thoughtfulness and empathy can help us be prudent and considerate of others as we trudge down this road to emotional freedom.

Amends need to be made even though we will feel uncomfortable.
It's a huge mistake to postpone making amends until we feel comfortable or because we think it's not the right time. Let's first deal with the idea that we should feel comfortable when making amends. We won't. In my opinion it's unrealistic to think we can face someone we have hurt and feel good about it. It's just not possible. If we possess a conscience, we are going to feel guilt and remorse. This is the purpose of a healthy conscience, but because our conscience interfered with our addiction, we became very good at rationalizing rotten behavior or numbing our guilt or remorse. We knew when we did something that was wrong, but we didn't let that stop us.

Because we avoided discomfort, we haven't integrated our conscience into our functioning; therefore, we have to reacquaint ourselves with our conscience and learn how to honor and respect it. Feeling uncomfortable when we face someone we hurt is an appropriate response to the situation. So don't avoid making amends because it makes you uncomfortable. Be willing to endure the pain and guilt to resolve unfinished business. This is critical to our recovery. We need to face those we hurt with courage, discipline, and a willingness to go to any lengths to make them whole. Remember, it is the best in us that faces the worst in us.

We also need to be thoughtful about where and when we approach people to make our amends. We don't want to approach them when they are celebrating their birthday, or graduating, or during some other festive or important occasion. Why? Because we want to be considerate of their feelings and avoid doing more harm. Our selfishness and self-centeredness were at the root of our problem. Now, in recovery, we must learn to think of others too.

Requesting a special meeting may help you avoid evoking a painful memory at an inappropriate time. In this way, we can be certain we are not going to ruin a special occasion because we want to clear our conscience. It's also a good idea to make our amends at a location that provides a degree of privacy. We may want to provide a space where the person we've harmed can process his or her reaction without fearing public embarrassment if he or she starts to cry or get angry. The exception to this consideration is if you have intimidated and frightened someone in the past. Then you want to take extra measures to ensure that he or she feels safe meeting you.

Be Sincere and Willing to Go to Any Lengths to Make Someone Whole

In Step 8, we became willing to make amends to those people we have harmed. Step 9 is about being sincere when we make amends. We are trying to restore social justice. What does this mean? It means that we restore the human rights of a person whom we have violated. If we are genuinely sincere, there is a chance that our amends will promote healing and make someone whole again.

We need to face the pain we have caused others. If we have harmed a child or children, we interfered with their physical, emotional, and/or spiritual development. We stole from them a safe atmosphere in which to grow and develop. If we wounded a partner, spouse, or parent, we caused them hardship, grief, anxiety, depression, insecurity, low self-esteem, or fear. Betrayal, cruelty, boundary violations, selfishness, and insincerity cause physical illnesses, emotional disorders, and spiritual wounds.

Being sincere when we make amends is the result of putting the best in us in charge of this task—the part of us that has empathy and compassion for those we have hurt so we can begin to glimpse the pain and suffering we have caused. Remember the Stanford Forgiveness Project that Dr. Luskin helped design? One of his observations was that, when a grievance is formed, our victims have taken what we have done to them personally. They also blame us for the feelings they struggle with and develop a narrative about what happened. When they retell the story, either silently to themselves or to others, it re-traumatizes them. It evokes the same physiological reactions they had when they were originally hurt. When we traumatize someone, we steal much joy from their lives. Instead of doing more enjoyable activities, they may spend their time struggling with their pain.

When we make amends, we must acknowledge how deeply we have wounded others. We must help them understand that what we did was not personal. They, our victims, were in no way responsible for what we had done to them. We cannot justify our rotten behavior. We did what we did because of who *we* were, not because of who *they* were. We must try to help them dispel the idea that what happened to them was personal. Conveying this point is especially important when we choose to make amends to a partner for being unfaithful.

We also must be willing to go to any lengths to make financial restitution or make whole those we have hurt. As a way to right a wrong, some of us have gone to jail to serve time for crimes we committed. Others have spent years making financial restitution to those they have stolen from. Some of us have paid for the therapy someone needed in order to address the emotional and spiritual damage we caused through our emotional or verbal abuse. The point is, we need to be willing to take total responsibility for our harmful actions and go to great lengths to restore social justice.

Our sincerity to face and make right the harm that we have done will be crucial in helping our victims begin the healing process. This can only be achieved if we are making amends for the right reason.

What, therefore, is the right reason? The answer is that *we have to make amends because it is the right thing to do rather than making amends because we are seeking forgiveness.* If we make amends to gain forgiveness, then we are manipulating the other person into doing what we want. That kind of manipulation simply inflicts more harm.

When we are sincere, forgiveness may come—or it may not. The point is that we cannot expect to be forgiven because we are humbling ourselves and taking responsibility for what we have done wrong. Our job is to make amends for the sake of our integrity, to restore social justice.

Keeping a hold on the right reason for making amends can help us respond appropriately whether we are forgiven or not. If we make amends for the right reason, then a victim's lack of forgiveness will not knock us off balance. We will give them room to respond in whatever way they need to. We will let them vent or tell us how they were hurt. We won't interrupt them or insist they are wrong. We will honor and respect their feelings.

We won't impose any expectations or impose any judgment on their response; we will accept their reaction for what it is. We may feel bad that we have not been able to restore their wholeness, but we will be at peace with the fact that we made amends because it was the right thing to do, regardless of the outcome. Please note: if we are manipulating our victims to forgive us so that we can feel less guilty, then we will react to their rejection with anger and resentment rather than compassion.

You are responsible for ensuring that your motivation to make amends is based on a genuine wish to right a wrong, rather than to be forgiven.

Don't Give Up If You Fail

I want to end my discussion of Step 9 by sharing a failure I had when making amends to a former employer, and how I was instructed to handle it.

I dropped out of high school at age sixteen because education was interfering with my drinking. The state of Illinois required that if I dropped out of school at age sixteen, I had to go to continuation school one day a week and get a job until I was seventeen years old.

The first job I had after dropping out of high school was selling women's shoes. This lasted for six months, and then I found a better job as a shipping and receiving clerk at an electronics store. Oscar owned the company, which sold and distributed electronic vacuum tubes for factories and television repair shops. It was a very successful business. He was a great boss, and he seemed to really like me. He often treated me like the son he never had, buying me lunch and giving me fatherly advice, such as telling me to go to college.

He respected me and my work ethic. I liked him and worked hard for him. My job was to fill the orders from our stock of tubes, pack them carefully, and ship them to the purchaser. While filling these orders, I noticed how expensive some of these tubes were. The prices ranged from a couple of dollars to several thousand dollars.

I was making a little bit more than minimum wage and spending most of my money on partying. I was an addict and needed more and more money to party with. I decided I'd fill an order of tubes and then sell them to acquire some extra spending cash. One day I filled up a box of about forty tubes and placed it in the Dumpster outside the rear door. That night I returned to the store and fished the box out of the trash.

The day after I stole the tubes, I realized that I had no idea how to sell them or who to sell them to. Back then, there was no Craigslist where I could post them. They just sat in my basement, gathering dust and reminding me of my guilt rather than financing my drinking. When I started working Step 8 after I was clean and sober for three months, I knew I had to put Oscar on my amends list. I didn't know if he'd ever noticed the tubes were missing, but it didn't matter. I knew that what I had done was wrong. That was all that counted.

My sponsor, Tom, and I came up with a plan on how to make amends to Oscar. It started by giving Oscar a call and asking to see him. He sounded really glad to hear from me. He invited me to join him for lunch and tell him about my time in the U.S. Marine Corps. I had stopped working for Oscar when I joined the armed forces in 1969. He was curious about my time serving our country, especially the time I spent in Vietnam (1970–71).

I dug the tubes out of the basement, put them in the front seat of my orange Volkswagen Bug, and drove to Oscar's store to make my amends. Here's where I made my first mistake: I left the tubes on the front seat of my Bug when I arrived and went inside the factory to meet with Oscar.

When I saw him, my stomach sank. He was so excited to see me; how could I tell him that I had stolen from him? How could I disappoint this man who thought so well of me? Making amends was becoming more difficult by the moment. And what happened at lunch made it even worse.

Over lunch, he told me he was proud of me for serving our country. He told me I was the best employee he ever had, that I was intelligent and a hard worker, and that I would be successful at whatever I chose for a career. At this point in our visit, I decided that this was one of those cases where making amends would do more harm than good. I aborted the mission. Wouldn't it hurt this man to tell him I had stolen the tubes? This clearly seemed to be a situation where it wasn't going to do any good to make amends.

I said good-bye to him and never discussed the real purpose for my visit. Later, I called Tom and tried to rationalize why I didn't make amends, but he didn't fall for it. He suggested that I didn't want to disappoint Oscar because of my ego and pride. I wasn't thinking about Oscar's feelings—I was thinking about my own. I didn't want to face the consequences of my behavior. Hasn't this always been what caused me problems in my relationships? He was right. It was. We came up with another plan.

I was to call Oscar and tell him that I would like to meet with him again but decline any offer to go to lunch. I was to ask him for a half hour of his time in his office. I was also told to walk into the factory with the tubes in my arms.

I followed Tom's directions and met with Oscar in his office. This was very hard for me. I was terribly anxious. I let Oscar know that during our first meeting I had wanted to make amends for stealing from him but lost the courage. I told him that I was in recovery for an alcohol and drug problem, and that an important part of my recovery was to make amends to the people that I had harmed. I put the tubes on his desk and told him that I had stolen them from him. I also let him know that I was terribly sorry for betraying him and that I was prepared to do whatever he wanted me to do to make restitution. If he felt like calling the police to report me, I would understand. If he wanted me to work for him until I had accounted for the money he lost, I would do that. I wanted him to know that I was willing to do whatever he needed me to do to make him whole.

Oscar was obviously hurt and upset. But he told me he was even more proud of me for having the courage to face him with my transgression. He said he forgave me and wished me all the best in my recovery. He said he didn't want to call the police or have me work for him. He wanted me to stay in school and get a college education. My restitution was in humbling myself before him. He smiled and said, "Take the tubes. I hope you can sell them and make a few bucks." He laughed; we laughed. I felt a tremendous relief and peace of mind.

Not all amends will go this well. But if you approach each of them with the right attitude, then regardless of what happens, you will be well on your way to emotional recovery and emotional well-being.

Resolving Unfinished Business

Each time we make amends, we resolve another piece of unfinished business. This has a very positive effect on our psyche. Here's what happens:

When a situation is unresolved, it requires a certain amount of our psychic energy to hold that situation in the background of our consciousness. Remember, unfinished business wants to push itself forward into our consciousness to get resolved. This is the cycle of experience I discussed in chapter 1. When we resolve something that was unresolved, we free up the energy that was used in holding the situation in the background of our mind. This energy now becomes available for living, for helping us deal more effectively with what's happening in the present moment.

Once we have made amends, we have given ourselves a new level of peace of mind and emotional well-being. Our job does not end here, however, lest we should regress. Recovery is like walking up an escalator that is going down. If we stop, we don't stand still—we regress. We must live according to what we know is right and good. We need to develop a practice of self-searching that will ensure that we hold on to the gains we have made in developing ego-integrity, emotional sobriety, and a more positive self-concept. Now that we have cleaned up our side of the street, we want to make sure we continue to keep our side of the street clean. We want to develop a practice that will help us maintain our integrity and trustworthiness.

Working Step 10

Step 10: Continued to take personal inventory and when we were wrong promptly admitted it.

Therapeutic Effect: Integrating self-examination, self-regulation, and emotional maturity into our daily lives.

If we were rigorous in making amends, we have forgiven ourselves for what we have done wrong and realized that we don't have to be perfect to be OK. We understand that being authentic and honest is more important than being perfect. We accept that we are a work in progress.

To continue maturing emotionally and spiritually, to continue realizing our human potential, we need to integrate what we have learned about ourselves and human relations into a new way of life. We need a practice that will continue to promote honest self-appraisal, self-awareness, self-regulation, and responsibility. We need a practice that will put the best of ourselves in charge of an ongoing self-examination and a prompt admission when we are wrong. Bill

Wilson noted the importance of such a practice when he said, "No one can make much of his life until self-searching becomes a regular habit, until he is able to admit and accept what he finds, and until he patiently and persistently tries to correct what is wrong" (*Twelve Steps and Twelve Traditions* 1981, 88).

Step 10 involves three different kinds of inventories that are distinguished from each other by their time factor. Here they are: (1) a Spot Check Emotional and Behavioral Inventory (SCEBI) that is designed to immediately get us back into sync with our fellows; (2) a Daily Emotional and Behavioral Inventory (DEBI) done at the conclusion of each day that is designed to remind us of what we are doing well and where we need improvement, and to admit when we are wrong; and (3) a regularly scheduled Recovery Progress Checkup (RPC). Let's explore each of these in some detail.

Spot Check Emotional and Behavioral Inventory (SCEBI)

We can think of the SCEBI as emotional first aid. Using this tool, we can recover our emotional balance before we react and make things worse. This inventory is taken whenever we are emotionally tangled up or upset, at any time of the day.

We use this SCEBI to figure out what is going on with us when we are upset or angry. The basis for this self-appraisal is found in an observation that Bill Wilson made. He claimed, "It is a spiritual axiom that every time we are disturbed, no matter what the cause, there is something wrong *with us*" (*Twelve Steps and Twelve Traditions* 1981, 90).

What is getting us upset? How do we figure out what is bothering us? We can apply the insights from Dr. Luskin's work on how grievances are formed. He found that we get upset when we take things personally and blame the other person for our feelings. If we are honest with ourselves, we can usually trace the origin of our reaction to an unenforceable rule that we have, that we demand someone adhere to, and that someone has violated.

Ask yourself the following question and fill in the blanks to help you discover your unenforceable rule. "If _____ (fill in the person) said or did _____ (fill in the words or action), I would feel _____ (fill in the feeling)." Here are a couple of examples to help you see how this works.

Example 1: Carly was upset with her boyfriend because he didn't reciprocate and say he loved her whenever she declared her love for him. Here's how Carly would fill out the incomplete sentence: "If my boyfriend said he loved me when I told him I loved him, I would feel loved and closer to him." Can you detect Carly's rule? Her rule was that he had to reciprocate when she told him she loved him in order for her to feel loved. This was her unenforceable rule. She made it seem like it was reasonable to ask him to respond in kind, when she was really manipulating him to do what she wanted him to do so that she would feel loved. When he didn't say he loved her, she felt insecure. She wanted him to behave the way she wanted him to so that she'd feel desirable rather than anxious and insecure.

Example 2: Harvey drove to Newport Beach to go to dinner with his sponsor and attend a meeting together. Dinner went well. They talked about Harvey's dissatisfaction with his current job and what he might consider doing about it. However, when they went to the AA meeting his sponsor sat with several other AA members whom he also sponsored. Harvey was upset. He felt rejected. If Harvey completed the sentence, he would say, "If my sponsor gave me all of his attention, I would feel important."

Can you figure out Harvey's rule? His unenforceable rule was that his sponsor had to behave the way he wanted him to in order for Harvey to feel important. Harvey thought that his request was reasonable; after all, he drove all the way to Newport Beach from Torrance, California, to spend time with him. It wasn't reasonable. It was an unenforceable rule. Harvey wanted to regulate how his sponsor behaved so that he would feel important. When his sponsor didn't adhere to his unenforceable rule, Harvey felt unimportant and hurt.

Our emotional dependency creates rules about how people are supposed to behave if they care about us. We typically impose these rules without much awareness that we are doing so. We camouflage our unreasonable demands to make them look reasonable. A wolf in sheep's clothing is still a wolf. We expect people to behave the way that we think they ought to. We demand that they do things the way we want them to so that we can feel OK. We try to regulate others because we don't know how to soothe our own anxieties and insecurities.

When we do the SCEBI and uncover our unenforceable rules, we need to promptly admit that we are wrong. We don't have the right to impose our rules on others. We have to unhook our self-esteem from what we expect other people to do to make us feel OK and stand on our own two feet. We need to become self-supporting. We need to validate ourselves. This is at the heart of emotional recovery and emotional maturity.

Daily Emotional and Behavioral Inventory (DEBI)

The DEBI is best taken at night. It is based on a review of the day that focuses on what we have done well and where we have not done so well. We need to be balanced in our self-appraisal. We are reconstructing our self-concept, and therefore we need to recognize what we have done well at the same time that we are evaluating where we need to admit a wrong or improve.

Some of the questions we need to ask ourselves are:

- When did I feel good about myself today?
- When was I part of the solution rather than the problem?
- When did I stop, pause, and reflect on what was going on before reacting?
- How did I improve a situation I was in?
- Was I selfish and self-serving?
- Was I dishonest?
- Was I honest and authentic in my interactions with others?
- Was I wrong but didn't admit it?
- Am I justifying or rationalizing an inappropriate behavior or reaction?

Feel free to add to this list. The point is that we are reviewing our day with the purpose of recognizing our progress and need for improvement.

Here's an example of Calvin practicing self-examination:

Calvin had been seeing me because he was having trouble in his relationship with his wife. She claimed that he had an anger problem. Calvin did often get angry with Eve. But the real problem that caused him to be so reactive and angry was that Calvin didn't know how to hold on to himself. He made Eve's opinion of him way too important.

Here's an instance that he described to me. Calvin and Eve had been out for dinner and had a great time. They felt very close to one another. Eve told him that she'd like to "get busy" after they put the children to bed. Calvin was ecstatic. Eve told Calvin she'd love to put on the new lingerie he bought for her on his last business trip. She said that she'd go upstairs, put the children to bed, brush her teeth, and put on the lingerie. Calvin decided to turn on the Olympics and wait for the green light. But instead of getting a green light, he got a red one. Eve shouted down the stairs to him with an irritated tone, "Where *are* you?" Calvin felt scolded and jumped off the couch and went upstairs to convince Eve that he didn't do anything wrong. (This is not the best approach to foreplay, in case you were wondering.)

Instead of making love, they started quibbling. Calvin tried to convince Eve that she was wrong and that he didn't do anything wrong. She wasn't accepting Calvin's explanation and held her position that he should have been upstairs waiting instead of watching the Olympics. When I asked Calvin how he felt about his behavior, he was fine with it. He wanted to give Eve the space to put the kids to bed. If he was up there with her, it would take much longer because they'd want him to read them a story. So he decided to wait downstairs. He didn't want Eve to be upset with him, so he tried to talk her out of her position. This led to more than an hour of quibbling. No sex—only quibbling.

When Calvin stepped back and examined his behavior, he discovered that he was too dependent on how Eve thought about him. He couldn't stand the thought of her being upset with him. It made him terribly anxious. He made her opinion of him more important than his own knowledge of his motivation.

If only he held on to himself better, he wouldn't need to convince her of anything. She could have her perception about him, and he could have his. He wouldn't need to quibble with her and convince her that she was wrong. Instead, he got angry when she wouldn't let him convince her that she was wrong. His manipulation didn't work, and he got frustrated. He tried to manipulate her in order to feel good about himself. He was trying to get her to support him, when what he really needed to do was support himself.

If Calvin had held on to himself, he would have jumped up from the couch and sprinted upstairs, focusing on being with his wife rather than manipulating her to validate him. Then they could have had some fun and enjoyed each other.

Calvin was able to recognize that the best in him was looking at the worst in him. He felt good that he was beginning to get honest with himself and his game playing. This was a great step forward in his maturity and in his recovery.

This daily practice can help us continue to keep the best in us in charge of our growth and development.

Recovery Progress Checkup (RPC)

This type of inventory focuses on the progress we have made in our recovery and is typically done annually or semiannually.

I met with a young man not long ago. For almost two years he was in my Executive Class Treatment Program, an individualized program for those who have failed at several of the more traditional recovery programs. His life was a mess when he first entered my program. His drinking and use of other drugs had put him in jail. I was able to get him released for treatment on what is called *alternative sentencing.*

He had alienated and was estranged from everyone in his family. He had no consideration or respect for anyone, and yet he expected everyone to show him consideration and respect. When things didn't go his way, he'd become angry and intimidating, making verbal threats of physical violence. The staff worked hard with him and struggled through many trying and scary times.

It had been over six months since we'd last met. He called me for an appointment, telling me he'd like to see me soon. During our meeting, he discussed several issues that were bothering him. As we talked, I commented on something that he wasn't saying but was implied in what he shared: he hadn't had an altercation with someone since December of the previous year. He stopped for a moment, saying he had goose bumps. He didn't realize that he had kept himself from creating drama. This was noteworthy progress. It was extremely important that he could see this change in his life. As we talked he also acknowledged that he was not beating himself up for not having a purpose in his life. He said it was great to acknowledge something wrong without berating himself for it. I smiled and acknowledged his pride in himself for making some real and tangible progress.

This is the value of a Recovery Progress Checkup. It can help us take stock of the progress we have made and identify the areas in our lives that need some tender loving care.

Summary
Steps 8 and 9 helped us restore trust and develop healthier relationships. We have learned to keep our side of the street clean rather than focus on what's wrong with others. We realized that we needed to change because it was the right thing to do. We shifted our center of emotional gravity back into ourselves and urged ourselves to do better for the sake of our own integrity. When we changed for the right reason, we saw that it was intrinsically rewarding. We started to validate ourselves.

By making amends to those people we have harmed, we recovered our integrity. We resolved unfinished business and freed up a lot of psychic energy trapped in unfinished business. We no longer had to endure a raging civil war in our guts. Our self-esteem improved, and we demonstrated that we were becoming trustworthy.

Step 10 helped us maintain our emotional maturity and integrate what we have learned about ourselves and healthy human relations in Steps 1–9. We have experienced a personal transformation. We are well on our way to reconstructing ourselves.

We have embarked on a major transformation of ourselves and

our attitudes. The path has been treacherous and challenging, but persistent and honest effort, along with a good guide and a power greater than ourselves, has helped us discover a new understanding of ourselves and a path to healthier human connections. We have started to incorporate a design for daily living in our lives that keeps us emotionally balanced, in harmony with our true-self and with others.

There are many hidden benefits, or rewards, from our efforts to adhere to right principles and healthier living. In the second part of this book, I will help you see some of the changes that you can expect from making amends and consistently practicing self-examination and self-regulation.

Part 2:

The Twelve Hidden Rewards
of Making Amends

Hidden Reward 1:
Staying in Close Contact with Our Experience

We hated feeling bad. We were phobic, always avoiding any pain or discomfort. We wanted life to be easy, and we would go to great lengths to maneuver away from any situation that might cause us anxiety or tension. Our first instinct was always to run. We'd do whatever was necessary to escape feeling uncomfortable. This fed our addiction like oxygen feeds a fire.

Working Steps 8, 9, and 10 have shown us that we are not as fragile as we once thought. We don't need to run away. We are discovering that we have an innate ability to experience discomfort and grow from it, and that pain is nothing more than a signal that something is wrong. If we have a broken leg and we try to walk on it, it's going to hurt. Our leg is saying, "Don't walk on me, I'm broken. I need rest and help."

Our pain has been trying to communicate with us for a long time, but we haven't been listening. We didn't want to hear what it was saying. We blocked out the message by anesthetizing ourselves, by not listening, by playing games—and we paid a huge price for our avoidance. We remained trapped in our emotionally immature behavior—imprisoned in a false-self. No one could trust us, and we couldn't even trust ourselves. Without a willingness to experience our painful feelings, we can never grow and mature into the person we'd like to be. We can never reach our potential. We can never grow into the person we were supposed to be. We can never become our true-self.

To grow, we must stay in close contact with our experience, whatever it is. This is one of the things we are learning when we work Steps 8, 9, and 10.

Our experience holds important information for our growth and development. We need to stay in close contact with how we behaved in our relationships in order to make a thorough list of those we have harmed. We must face the wrongs we have done without running away from the truth. Step 8 stops us from running, and has us hold still and feel our feelings.

If we were rigorously honest with ourselves while making the list of people we had harmed, we probably felt one or more of the following feelings: anxiety, shame, discomfort, or guilt. This is exactly what we were supposed to feel. We were learning that we don't have to feel comfortable to be OK. We can be uncomfortable and OK at the same time. In fact, another hidden reward is that the more willing we are to feel uncomfortable, the more comfortable we become. Yes, another paradox!

This process of learning from our pain also happens in Step 9. We have to stay in close contact with our experience as we humble ourselves before those we have hurt. We need to feel the pain and discomfort that comes from having violated our own moral and ethical standards. We need to stay in close contact with our experience to understand how we betrayed ourselves and others. This self-understanding is at the heart of self-forgiveness and emotional recovery.

Step 10 asks us to continue staying close to our experience and learning from it. We are asked to frequently engage in self-examination whenever we are upset or angry. We need to use the experience of our daily interactions and behavior in a regular practice. This practice is designed to show us where we need to give ourselves credit for handling a situation well, where we still need improvement, and where we needed to admit we were wrong. We need to stay close to our experience to make these spot checks and daily reviews of who we are and who we aren't.

We have recovered the ability to stay in close contact with our experience and to learn from it. This has restored our ability to flow with the cycle of experience. We just aren't getting in the way of ourselves as much as we used to, and when we do, we can become aware of how we are blocking ourselves and work through it.

Matt attended my retreat on emotional recovery. He had more than twenty years in NA and seemed to be working a solid program. Part of the retreat was spent completing the Emotional Sobriety Inventory Form provided in the appendix of my previous book *12 Smart Things to Do When the Booze and Drugs Are Gone.* The first column of this form required Matt to describe a situation that upset him. Here's what he talked about:

Two months earlier, he and his wife, Sheila, were planning on leaving for a thirty-day European cruise. He and Sheila had been looking forward to this cruise for more than a year. They were even upgraded to a first-class suite that came with its own butler. Matt was excited to be treated like royalty.

What attracted Matt and his wife to this particular cruise was that they would be dropped off with their road bikes and a guide in one of the Spanish ports, ride for a couple of days, and meet up with the ship in another port. Matt loved to ride, and so did his wife. He imagined how great it would be to ride through little Spanish villages, stop for lunch, and experience the beautiful countryside from the seat of his bike. Well, they never went on the trip. Sheila fell down a flight of stairs and broke her leg three weeks before they planned to leave. Good thing they had bought vacation insurance.

Matt was upset. He unconsciously blamed Sheila for ruining the trip. He would scold her and tell her that she should have been more careful. He'd tell her that she ruined his summer. He made it all about him.

Matt was terribly disappointed, but he didn't know how to soothe himself and lick his own wounds; instead, he verbally lashed out at Sheila. I could see that there was a part of Matt that wasn't feeling good about his behavior, but he wouldn't admit that he was wrong.

Matt justified how he was treating Sheila. After all, he thought, she was a bit careless. She needed to be more careful, and it was his job to straighten her out. As he discussed in our session what happened, he made a passing comment to the group that he wasn't being very compassionate toward her. I interrupted him and said, "You're worse than that, Matt. Not only are you not being compassionate, you are also being sadistic and beating her up because you are disappointed!" Wow, that stopped Matt in his tracks. He knew it was true. Immediately, he started feeling remorseful for his selfish and cruel behavior. He realized that Sheila felt disappointed too, but there was no room for her feelings—it was all about Matt.

Here's a snapshot of the dialogue that happened next:

Dr. Berger: It's time for you to work Step 10 with her, Matt.

Matt: You're right, but won't she hate me?

Dr. Berger: You don't have to worry about that—she already thinks you're a jerk.

Matt (sarcastic): Thanks.

Dr. Berger: The only thing that she doesn't know is that there is a part of you that *knows* you're a jerk and wants to be better than that. I'm certain she'd love to get to know that about you as well.

Matt (smiling): Yes, I guess she does know that I'm a jerk. I guess I need to make amends, don't I?

Dr. Berger: You guess?

Matt: OK, I need to make amends. Wow, I can really feel a resistance to the idea. There's a part of me that doesn't want to admit I'm wrong.

Matt stayed in close contact with his experience as we explored his resistance. He learned a lot about himself and how his selfishness hurt his relationship. He came to see how his false-self made it very hard for him to admit when he was wrong. Matt made a commitment to the group to work Step 10 when he got home. The week after the retreat was over, I got a call from Matt. He told me that he had made amends to his wife and it worked out better than he could have imagined.

One of the many hidden rewards in working Steps 8, 9, and 10 is to stay in close contact with our experience so we can learn from it. Let's now unpack the second hidden reward that comes from making amends.

Hidden Reward 2:
Authenticity

Steps 8, 9, and 10 show us how much we have to gain by being authentic. These three Steps provide us with an opportunity to experience our potential self—our authentic-self. We see that we are much more than the self we became in order to manage our anxiety and control life. This fabricated-self limited our possibilities because it prohibited us from staying in close contact with our experience. It forced us to play roles. It created a caricature of a person. We became masters at manipulation and deception. We were inhuman and cruel.

Our false-self determined that some ways of being were OK and others were not. We disowned parts of ourselves so we could live according to its perfectionist demands and specifications. There was no room for us to be our authentic-self under the reign of this tyrant. We were exiled from our own life. Isn't that absurd? No wonder we had so many problems. No wonder we were lost and empty. When we denied our authentic self to meet unreal expectations, we disconnected ourselves from the best in ourselves in favor of the worst in ourselves.

Steps 8, 9, and 10 reunite us with our true-self. They help us put the best in us in charge. They require that we use our self-understanding and insight into our character defects to right our wrongs. By taking responsibility for the harm we have caused and sincerely making amends, we start to experience serenity and peace of mind.

By stepping up, owning who we really are, and taking responsibility for our actions, we continue the reconstruction of a more positive self-concept. Fritz Perls (1969), the founder of Gestalt therapy, stated, "Authenticity, maturity, responsibility for one's actions and life, response-ability, and living in the now, having the creativeness of the now available, is all one and the same thing." Authenticity is central to our growth and development. It is essential to our recovery and to our maturity.

We must persistently try to reveal ourselves as we are in this moment, without censorship, if we are to reconstruct our lives and increase our self-esteem. We will discuss this in more detail later. For now, it's important to note that honesty and authenticity catalyze and initiate the process of change. Remember, the paradoxical theory of change tells us that change occurs when we own who we are and what we are doing, rather than by trying to be someone we are not.

Being authentic means revealing your truth—your experience. Authenticity is an intention to reveal yourself as you are in this moment. Without authenticity, we cannot be trustworthy or have deep, meaningful, intimate relationships. The word *intimacy* comes from the Latin word *intimus,* meaning "innermost." To be intimate we must be willing to reveal our innermost experience and truth.

Authenticity is also critical if we are going to benefit from a practice of inward searching and self-examination. If we don't admit to our innermost self what we know to be the truth, then we are still playing games, avoiding ourselves, and being selectively honest. This will mess up our efforts at creating a better life. Selective honesty is one of the many ways that we can sabotage our recovery. (If you'd like to learn more about the effects of selective honesty on recovery, see Stupid Thing 4 in *12 Stupid Things That Mess Up Recovery*.)

Finally, authenticity creates presence. It allows us to live in the moment, right here, right now. When we are present, we are fully experiencing ourselves, our thoughts, our feelings, and the other person. We are fully aware of what is happening in the moment.

Fernando had one hundred days sober, and over six months without a cigarette. He was amazed at what a difference being sober made in how he experienced himself. When he was drinking, his family often confronted him about his hot temper. It didn't take much for him to blow a gasket, which alienated and estranged his wife and children. They walked on eggshells around him, being careful not to say or do something that would cause him to erupt. He held the entire family hostage with his anger, but he denied that he had an anger problem. After all, they were the ones who screwed up and needed to be held accountable for their actions. He blamed them for his angry outbursts.

I hadn't seen Fernando for a couple of months. He called me and told me that he and his wife needed an appointment as soon as possible. He opened the psychotherapy session by discussing what he was learning about himself. He was starting to realize that his family was right: he was angry, at least most of the time. He was baffled by how strong and persistent his anger was, even though he was trying to manage it better. He turned to his wife and sincerely apologized for how he had treated her and the children. He told her that he must have created hell for them. He was clearly upset with himself.

When I asked Fernando to elaborate about what he was experiencing, he said he was beginning to see that he treated his family in the same way his father had treated him, his siblings, and his mother. His father wanted to have complete control over each of them and everything they did. This is not who Fernando wanted to be. "Father knows best" was the philosophy that his father had used to inflict his sadistic control on the family. Fernando was now admitting that he was doing the same thing.

He asked his wife if she would support him when he asked his children to join him in a family session so that he could make his amends. He wanted her to encourage their children to attend. She agreed.

When they got home, he asked his children to join him in the next session. His wife gladly supported him in front of the children. This was a very different dynamic, and their children weren't quite certain what to make of it. Initially, they were cynical and distrustful. Fernando's wife had previously aligned herself with the children in a parent-child coalition to protect the children from his alcoholism and anger. Now she was supporting him because he was taking responsibility for how he had harmed the family.

Fernando showed up the following week with his children. You can probably imagine how emotional and healing the three hours we spent were as he made amends for his alcoholism and anger. Because he was more present and willing to take responsibility for his inappropriate behavior, his children started to feel better about him, thinking he might be a safe person for them to open up to. Each of his three children shared with him openly and honestly about their feelings toward him. His authenticity invited them to be real with him, and they were. They told him about specific situations where he terrorized the entire family. They told him that they disrespected him and were going to use him as an example of how not to parent when they had kids of their own. They cried as they allowed themselves to feel the reality of what their family had been through. Fernando cried too.

He made amends and told them that he had a deep compassion for them and what they were feeling because this was how he felt as a child too. His authenticity, sincerity, and willingness to make amends for his harmful behavior started the healing for the entire family. They were being restored to wholeness. They were recovering their family life and their relationship with each other.

Authenticity is an incredible gift and reward for having the courage to face ourselves as we are, warts and all. It also helps us connect to a deep compassion for our own suffering, for the suffering we have caused others, and for those who are still suffering. Let us turn our attention to the next hidden reward of making amends, the development of genuine, heartfelt compassion.

Hidden Reward 3:
Compassion and Forgiveness

Working Steps 8, 9, and 10 opens us up to feeling compassion, acting compassionately, and forgiving ourselves and others. This is another hidden reward of working these three Steps.

A spirit of compassion evolves from the process of making amends and from a practice of self-examination. Being compassionate is a natural outcome of this process. By making a list of all the people we have harmed and discovering the pattern underlying our hurtful behavior, we can see that we were the common denominator in all our difficulties. We need to stop deflecting responsibility for what went wrong in our lives and instead gain insight into our own role in our problems.

To ensure this will be a therapeutic exercise, we must rise above blame and be honest with ourselves about what we have done. We have to take responsibility for who we are and who we are not. We have to realize that we are imperfect, that we are in need of help, and that making mistakes doesn't mean that we *are a mistake.* God doesn't make any junk!

We need to see that we were misinformed, misled, and ignorant, not that we are bad. We were lost in our false-self and all of its nonsense. We were lost in our addiction; our brain was hijacked. We became a fabricated-self that was designed to support a life based on unreasonable expectations and perfectionism. This is the source of self-compassion.

Taking responsibility for who we have been, what we have done wrong, and who we want to be is self-empowering. We cannot make sincere amends unless we are compassionate. The meaning of the word *compassion* demonstrates its importance in this process. It is derived from the Latin word *com,* which is a prefix that means "together," and *pati,* a suffix that means "to suffer." Compassion, therefore, is sorrow for the sufferings or trouble of someone, accompanied by the urge to help.

When we make amends, we engender compassion for ourselves and others. We come to see how we have harmed others. We face the worst in us with the best in us. Facing what we have done wrong and how we have hurt others will move us to feel remorse and appropriate guilt. We must not run away from these feelings; they are important. Guilt is the pain we feel after doing something that violates our own personal values and ethics. As we sit with the pain caused by our hurtful actions, a desire or urge to help ourselves and others will emerge. This desire motivates us to make amends and take responsibility for our actions. We become motivated to be the voice for social justice. We become motivated to restore wholeness to our victims and to ourselves. We become motivated to right our wrongs, to forgive and be forgiven.

What is forgiveness? Let us first discuss what it is not. Forgiveness is not condoning inappropriate or unkind behavior in ourselves or others. It is not letting ourselves off the hook, or letting others off the hook, nor is it a get-out-of-jail-free card. It is not forgetting what happened or looking the other way. Forgiveness doesn't always repair a relationship. It isn't the same as reconciliation or validation. Forgiveness isn't turning what we have done into something that is right.

Forgiveness is freeing. It is working through our feelings and seeing things from a different perspective. Forgiveness is a process that involves certain steps. First, we stop taking things personally and realize that people do unkind and hurtful things because of who *they* are, not because of who *we* are. This applies to our own inappropriate and harmful behavior as well. We were unkind and hurtful; no one caused us to be that way. We need to stop rationalizing and justifying our rotten behavior or the rotten behavior of others. Forgiveness helps us evict someone who has been taking up space in our minds rent-free. Working Steps 8, 9, and 10 also moves us out of the space we have occupied in the minds of those we have hurt.

Second, we take responsibility for our feelings. Forgiveness involves moving beyond blaming other people for what we feel. It involves taking responsibility for how we have behaved and responded. Remember, our happiness or emotional well-being is a result of the relationship we have to the experience we are having. It is not determined by the experience or trauma we have suffered.

The final step in the forgiveness process is about recovering our integrity. It is about developing a new narrative about what happened. It is about becoming a hero rather than a victim.

Dr. Luskin defined it this way: "Forgiveness is the feeling of peace that emerges as you take your hurt less personally, take responsibility for how you feel, and become a hero instead of a victim in the story you tell. Forgiveness is the experience of peacefulness in the present moment" (2002, 68).

I found Dr. Luskin's observations to be consistent with the ideas I discussed about emotional sobriety in *12 Smart Things to Do When the Booze and Drugs Are Gone*. Emotional sobriety is about not taking things personally and not letting other people's limited perceptions of us define us. Not coincidentally, this is also the key to forgiveness.

Forgiveness happens when we take our hurt less personally and take total responsibility for our reaction to the situation. This is impossible if we are emotionally dependent; our emotional dependency made us highly vulnerable to the behavior or actions of others. As we grow up emotionally and learn to stand on our own two feet, we learn to support ourselves: we become less reactive and less vulnerable to the unkind or hurtful behavior of others.

Let me give you an example of the power of forgiveness. Nathan was a fifty-nine-year-old man who was married with three children. He was a nurse and was currently on disability because of a bad back. Fifteen years earlier, he was caught stealing a patient's Demerol at the hospital. He subsequently entered treatment and had been clean and sober since that time.

Nathan came to see me after doing a considerable amount of work processing the abuse he experienced as a child. He was still haunted by his father's abusive behavior. A curious characteristic of Nathan was his hatred of vegetables: he never ate them, and they made him nauseated whenever he was close enough to smell them. This hatred grew directly from the abuse he had experienced. When Nathan was a child, his father demanded that he eat all of his vegetables. Nathan described a common scene at the dinner table. His father would lecture him on the health benefits of vegetables and why Nathan should eat every one of them on his plate. When Nathan would tell his father that he didn't like them, his father would reply that it didn't matter what he liked, he had to eat his vegetables. When Nathan refused, his father would get up from his chair and cross the room like some vicious predator approaching its helpless prey.

He'd grab Nathan by the back of his hair, pull his head back, scoop up a handful of vegetables from Nathan's plate, and stuff them in his mouth. He'd cover Nathan's nose to force him to open up his mouth and swallow the vegetables. While this madness was unfolding, Nathan's mother would be screaming at her husband to leave Nathan alone. But his father wouldn't stop manhandling Nathan. He demanded complete submission to his sadistic behavior. Nathan would struggle valiantly against his father's grip, but to no avail. Finally, Nathan would submit and swallow the vegetables, but then throw them up—sometimes all over his father, who would then beat Nathan for vomiting all over him.

Nathan had worked through the first step of forgiveness, which was to stop taking his father's behavior personally. He realized that his father did what he did because he was a sadistic man who was also abused by his own father. This helped somewhat, but Nathan's pain was still unresolved. He still blamed his father for his own unassertiveness. He felt like his father stole his power by demanding his submission and beating him into a state of helplessness and powerlessness.

In our session, I asked Nathan to imagine his father sitting in an empty chair beside him, and to let his father know what he had done to his son. Nathan looked at the chair and said, "You are a cruel bastard. You had no right to stuff my mouth with vegetables and force me to eat them. I have a right to say that I don't want to eat something." He then changed chairs and played his father: "No, you don't have any rights. I will tell you what rights you have and what rights you don't have. I am in control of you and what you do!"

I asked Nathan to shuttle back to the other chair and respond as himself. He said, "No you can't make me like vegetables. You can stuff them in my mouth, but you can't make me digest them and like it. I don't like vegetables, and I never will. I will vomit them all over you if you put them in my mouth!"

Nathan didn't realize what he had just said. I told him to repeat that last line and listen carefully to himself. He repeated what he said, "I don't like vegetables, and I never will. I will vomit them all over you if you put them in my mouth!"

A very different look came over his face. He smiled and turned to me and commented, "He couldn't make me like them and digest them, could he?"

"No, he couldn't," I told him. "You kept your integrity the best way you could. You were a very brave young man!"

Nathan was blown away, and he began to cry. He never thought of himself as being brave and as having any power, but he did. His father couldn't totally dominate him. Nathan's vomiting was the way he stood up to his father; it was his opposition and defiance. Nathan felt great about seeing himself in this light. At that moment, he stopped being his father's victim and instead became a hero. He changed the narrative—he changed the story he told himself and no longer needed to blame his father for his own unassertiveness. At long last, he had taken the final step in the process of forgiveness.

Forgiveness released Nathan from his painful past. I saw him a month after our session, and he told me he felt more powerful than he had ever felt before. He said, "I have finally forgiven my father."

Seeking to right our wrongs and take responsibility for what we have done wrong also releases us from our need to be right. We can end conflict with our fellows. We can stop trying to convince others that we are right and they are wrong. We can find a place beyond right and wrong to meet and heal, to restore our integrity and our victims' wholeness. Once we've forgiven those who have harmed us and are free of the burden of carrying it for so long, we experience the next hidden reward: autonomy and emotional freedom.

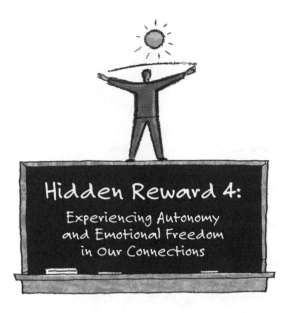

Hidden Reward 4:

Experiencing Autonomy
and Emotional Freedom
in Our Connections

Working Steps 8, 9, and 10 gives us many gifts. We stay in closer contact with our experience, we are more open and authentic, we develop more compassion and forgiveness than we have ever had for ourselves and others, and we are empowered by a better source of energy, by a higher power and a higher self. We no longer try to live up to a set of impossible standards that we imposed on ourselves in order to feel OK. Isn't it interesting that our original solution to our anxiety created hell on earth for ourselves and our loved ones? It didn't make us OK; it turned us into a juggernaut of destruction fueled by self-will run riot.

To unravel this mess, we had to let go of our old ideas and replace them with new ones that are rooted in reality. We had to let go of our fantasies of how we should be or how life should be in order to embrace the reality of the life we created. This wasn't a pleasant task. No one among us wants to see our mistakes projected on an IMAX screen in living color, but we must. We have to get honest with ourselves, or we won't change. We need to endure the pain and discomfort of gut-wrenching honesty. If we endure this pain, we begin to build a new life based on who we really are rather than playing some phony games—a new life that is based on authenticity.

The biggest game we played was manipulating our environment and everyone in it to do for us what we couldn't do for ourselves. This is what kept us immature. We expected people to act the way we wanted them to, to satisfy our needs for security, power, love, or approval. We expected situations to unfold the way we wanted them to so that we could feel good about ourselves. We were masters at manipulation and camouflaging our tricky behavior to make it seem like we were reasonable, but we weren't. We were unreasonable, demanding, and outrageous.

To survive and to satisfy our needs in life, we need to make contact with our environment and the people in it. This is the purpose of the cycle of experience I introduced you to in chapter 1. We are not an island of self-sufficiency. We need things from our environment—such as oxygen, food, shelter, and love—in order to survive. If we interact with our environment authentically, we won't play games to meet our needs. We will be clear about what we want, and see what we have to do to satisfy our needs. We won't need to manipulate others into doing our bidding.

We won't demand that things go our way. Once we grow up and mature, our interactions with others will be straightforward, respectful, authentic, honest, clean, and mutually satisfying. They won't be messy or dirty because they won't be riddled with expectations and rules. We won't be trying to manipulate others to do for us what we aren't doing for ourselves.

This rarely happened before we started working the Steps. We usually tried manipulating the world to give us what we didn't know how to give to ourselves. If we didn't feel lovable, then we demanded that other people act toward us in a manner that made us feel desirable. If we didn't feel secure, then we demanded that they make us feel safe. If we didn't feel smart, then we looked to others to make us feel intelligent. The list goes on and on. Our partners had to jump through hoops to make us feel that we were OK. This is emotional dependency, and it's the underlying force that turned us into control freaks and master manipulators.

And, ultimately, it didn't work. Emotional dependency made our self-esteem dependent on others. Our partner had to say this or do this or that to make us feel OK. Dr. Nathaniel Branden, an expert on self-esteem, described the effects of low self-esteem as an "excessive preoccupation with gaining the approval and avoiding the disapproval of others, hungering for validation and support at every moment of our existence" (1981, 84). Please hear this: it is not our partner's job or anyone else's job to make us feel OK. That is *our* job.

When we strive to validate ourselves, when we strive to stand on our own two feet, we become self-supporting. This means that we take responsibility for how we feel and what we want. We take responsibility for our self-esteem. We don't make it someone else's job to make us feel OK about ourselves—we take the responsibility to do what's needed to feel OK on our own.

Steps 8, 9, and 10 show us the path to self-validated self-esteem. These Steps encourage us do the right thing *because it is the right thing to do*, not because we are going to get validation or forgiveness from others. These Steps help us reclaim our emotional center of gravity. We stand for ourselves, balanced on our own two feet.

We make a list of those we have harmed because we want to be a better person—to validate ourselves. We make amends to take responsibility for our side of the street because it's the right thing to do, and we do it to forgive ourselves rather than to seek or receive forgiveness. We examine ourselves and admit when we're wrong because we're aiming at becoming the best person we can be—we do it because this is who we want to be.

When we become self-validating, we experience autonomy. We become our own person. We determine what is right for us. We stop living up to other people's expectations and become more concerned with what we expect from ourselves. We stop pressuring other people to change in order to make us feel OK, and instead look at what we need to change in ourselves. We stop telling other people that they need to listen to us, and we start to listen to ourselves.

As we achieve greater autonomy, we become less controlled by our anxieties and fears. We become less ruled by our emotional dependency, and therefore we become less controlling and manipulative. We begin to experience freedom in our relationships: with others and with ourselves. We become free to be ourselves, to speak our mind, to be authentic, to follow our own directives, and to face our wrongs and promptly admit them. We don't need to play games. We take responsibility for what we want, and we stop manipulating others.

Autonomy pertains to our capacity for self-direction and self-regulation. Nathaniel Branden (1981) attributed the following characteristics to a person who has achieved autonomy:

- understands that other people do not exist merely to satisfy his or her needs
- knows that no matter how much love or caring exists between us, we are, each of us, responsible for ourselves
- has outgrown the need to prove himself or herself as a good person
- doesn't need to turn someone into his or her mother or father
- doesn't need to be rescued or saved
- doesn't require permission to be himself or herself

- recognizes that self-worth resides within, and therefore his or her self-esteem is stable and not dependent on others
- has the ability to "roll with the punches" and be flexible and resilient
- respects his or her partner's need to follow their own truth or destiny
- recognizes that separateness is a dimension of a relationship, not a threat to it
- recognizes that we are evolving individuals. (136)

Branden's list suggests that as we mature emotionally, we are able to stand on our own two feet. We experience emotional freedom and become free to be ourselves. Because we took action to right our wrongs, to restore social justice, to practice honest self-evaluation, and to promptly admit when we were wrong, we have developed a more positive self-concept. Our self-esteem improves and we become more autonomous in our ability to function. We move into Stage II recovery and begin to cultivate healthier human relations. We are beginning to actualize our human potential. What an incredible gift!

Ashton was referred to me by his wife, who had read my book *12 Stupid Things That Mess Up Recovery*. She thought I might be able to help her husband with his drinking problem. Ashton had been seeing a psychologist who had been trying to help him drink in moderation, but the intervention failed. Of course it did: he was an addict, and addiction changes our brain. We lose the ability to regulate our drinking or using, and that modification to our brain is irreversible. His wife was desperate. Something had to change. She was on the verge of leaving him if he didn't stop drinking and if things between them didn't improve.

Although they lived in another part of the country, they were willing to fly in and spend a weekend working with me. The weekend was very intense; much work was done. What stood out, in addition to Ashton's alcoholism, was his emotional dependency. He hesitated to say anything in our conjoint sessions if he imagined his wife wouldn't like what he had to say. He was terrified of being rejected, which made him very cautious and hesitant in his communication and in his ability to respond authentically to her. He wouldn't dare anger her, and yet his unassertive behavior was driving her crazy. In her words, she wanted her husband "to step up and be a man." It wasn't exactly clear at that time what she wanted from him, and she couldn't clarify it when asked. But I knew we would figure it out along the way.

I educated Ashton about his alcoholism and the fact that he was powerless. We explored his drinking history, and it became undeniably clear that he was powerless over alcohol and that his life had become unmanageable. He accepted these facts and began regularly attending AA meetings and taking Antabuse on a daily basis.

Eventually drinking was no longer an issue, but he still couldn't step up and be present in his marriage. His wife kept telling him, "I need you to be strong." What she really meant was that she wanted him to be *present*. His emotional dependency kept him from showing up and participating in their relationship. He didn't dare disagree with her or challenge her even when he thought differently. He would always accommodate her position.

She was even more upset because she had believed all along that it was Ashton's *drinking* that prevented him from showing up in their relationship. But after he quit drinking, it became clear that something beyond alcohol was thwarting him: his emotional immaturity. The anxiety and fear that he wouldn't be loved kept him from being an equal participant in their relationship. He was afraid that his true-self was unlovable.

We set to work on addressing his emotional dependency. I made him aware of how powerful this force was in his life. I had him dialogue with the part of him that was afraid to assert itself and risk rejection or criticism. He was starting to see who he was and who he wasn't, and he realized that he too didn't like the part of himself that was emotionally immature.

Ashton started working the AA program, and when he got to Step 8 he realized that he had done to his wife what he had feared she was going to do to him: he abandoned her. This awareness helped him reach the critical mass he needed in order to change, and he imploded. He felt terrible, and in our conjoint session that day he turned to his wife and made his amends. He sobbed at how he had abandoned her in their relationship. He owned that he had let his fear and anxiety stop him from being the man he wanted to be. He made amends for not being present and for hiding out in the bottle. His wife softened tremendously. Her anger and hardness had come from the fact that she had been trying to run the family all by herself. She hadn't been able to count on him, but now that he was showing up she could let her defenses down.

Ashton has much more autonomy in his marriage because of the work he did to grow up and stand on his own two feet. Today, their relationship is much better than it has been for many years. There is no longer talk of divorce, and Ashton is much more authentic and real. He has recovered his true-self.

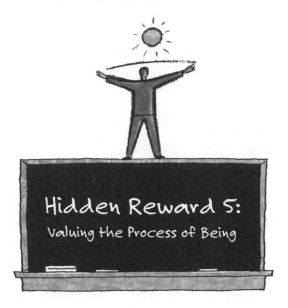

Hidden Reward 5:
Valuing the Process of Being

When we work Steps 8, 9, and 10, we gain a whole new perspective on life. We shift our thinking dramatically. We become more focused on who we are rather than on what we have. This represents a major shift in our psyche. The false-self was based on a notion of "the more I have, the more I am." We measured our worth in terms of our power, our real or imagined success, our knowledge, our jobs, our cars, our looks, our homes, or our bank accounts. Our worth was measured by what we had, not who we were. We lost sight of the importance of character and personal values and ethics.

Because our self-worth was determined by what we possessed, there could never be enough of what we thought we needed. We always wanted more, and we were driven to succeed in whatever terms became important to us. If we focused on our career, we were driven to be the best. If we focused on our looks, we were driven to compulsively exercise, starve ourselves, or get plastic surgery to make us more beautiful or handsome. If we were driven by power, we were compulsively driven to win. We were never satisfied because we believed that there was always more, and that more would be better. I'm certain you've heard addiction defined as "one is too much and a thousand isn't enough."

This brings to mind a very poignant moment in my recovery that I want to share with you.

My journey in recovery started on the Kaneohe Marine Corps Base on the island of Oahu, Hawaii, in 1971. I was a Vietnam veteran (1970–71) who returned from war with a serious drug addiction. Serendipity caused me to be the third marine admitted into an amnesty program that allowed Vietnam vets to receive treatment for their drug problem rather than discharging them from the Corps or prosecuting them under the Code of Military Justice.

Shortly after I entered treatment, I met the second marine who was admitted to the program. His name was Bill B., and we became instant friends. Bill was a unique-looking red-headed guy with lots of freckles, and everyone liked him. He was very popular with the girls and drove them crazy. I envied this in Bill because I always felt uncomfortable with women.

He was charismatic, funny as hell, and a hippie in Marine Corps fatigues. Before joining the Corps, Bill had been the drummer in a very popular psychedelic rock band in Southern California. Bill was a vet who became addicted primarily to heroin while in Vietnam, but he used other drugs as well.

Bill and I both got turned on to recovery, and we did everything together. We went to AA meetings together, we went to concerts together, we exercised together, and we ate chow together. We had the same sponsor, Tom, whom I mentioned earlier. We didn't own a car, so we got around the base and the nearby town, Kailua, on ten-speed bikes.

The two of us hung out with Tom and worked the Twelve Steps

together. We were brothers in recovery. We cried together, opened up our emotional wounds together, and started to heal together. Later, we were both asked to be counselors at the Drug Center, and we both accepted.

This was an amazing time in the field of recovery. Our program was a relatively new endeavor for the Marine Corps, and Bill and I had no real idea of what we were doing as counselors. Neither of us had any formal training, but we made up for what we didn't know with our passion for recovery, and with our commitment and willingness to go to any lengths to help the marine who was still suffering from his addiction.

Part of the Drug Center's philosophy was that we lived by the same principles we were teaching others. This meant that we confronted each other, in our staff meetings, about our games or dishonesty. Staff meetings were always exciting and scary. We didn't know whether we'd be put on the hot seat and confronted about something.

Well, one day it was my turn on the hot seat. Bill turned to me and said, "Have you noticed how you always have to ride in front of me? That you always take the lead? What's up with that, Berger?" He had busted me, and I was humiliated.

He was right: I wanted to win, to be first. I was competitive, and my false-pride fed off these small victories. I didn't care how this made Bill feel; all that mattered was that it boosted my ego. I hated that this part of me was exposed. I was in a double bind: I wanted to win, but I didn't want anyone to know that that was my motivation. I thought wanting to win was bad, so I had to hide it. I was ashamed of it. I played a game with myself and with others, trying to hide who I really was and mask the real motivation for my behavior: that there was a part of me that wanted to win—all the time—in order to feel superior.

Once I owned that this is what I was doing, something in me

changed. I realized I didn't need to win all the time. That part of me lost control. I started to see that my self-esteem was based on all the wrong things, like winning and having.

Working Steps 8, 9, and 10 helped me see that who I am is at least as important as what I have or what I've achieved. I started to find balance in my life.

One of the hidden rewards of working these three Steps is that our focus on outcomes diminishes. It is a paradox. When we shift our focus from outcomes to the challenges and joys of *being* (of process), we can use our awareness to realize our potential. Some of the outcomes we seek may actually happen, but what is more important is our attention to the *process of being*, rather than to goals. Carl Rogers (1961), one of the fathers of humanistic psychology, noted that when people grow in therapy they become able to flow with and follow their experience: we learn to move "toward being a process of potentialities being born, rather than being or becoming some fixed goal" (172).

Being a process of potentialities being born is exciting, because it is the process of uncovering and discovering who we really are. This reunites us with our true-self, with our basic need to grow, and restores our ability to self-actualize. We recover our motivation to grow, which was hijacked by our false-self and our addict-self.

By working Steps 8, 9, and 10, we are creating a more positive self-concept based on integrity and honesty. We are given the gift of being able to choose not to focus exclusively on outcomes, and instead shift our focus toward giving our best effort and being our best possible self. We can't control outcomes, but we can regulate our effort and attitude. This is one of many things that we learn by working Steps 8, 9, and 10. We learn to do the right thing because doing the right thing is valuable in itself, regardless of what we gain from it.

Hidden Reward 6:
Being Trustworthy

One of the hidden rewards from working Steps 8, 9, and 10 is the restoration of trust. We restore the trust we have shattered by becoming trustworthy. Being worthy of trust is critical if we are going to develop healthy human relations. Please note that I am focusing on *being trustworthy* in this section, not *trusting*. But before I unpack this issue of trustworthiness, I want to make a few comments about trust.

Trust is defined as complete confidence in the honesty, integrity, reliability, and justice of another person or thing. When we think of being with someone we trust, we feel safe. Herein lies the problem with trust: trust is mistakenly thought of as unilateral, or one-way. "If you fulfill my needs or my expectations, I can trust you and I'm comfortable being around you."

Trust is not something that is unilaterally determined in a relationship. Trust, true trust, is something that is co-created in our relationships. It is a result of what happens at the point of contact between two people. Real trust is grounded in facing the reality of who each of us is without needing to distort it or deny what we are seeing or experiencing. Trust must be grounded in who we are, what we are doing, and what is happening between us.

Trust is the experience that comes from how we reach or engage each other, and how we negotiate our level of intimacy. Contrary to social convention, trusting someone who is not trustworthy is not a virtue. It is foolish and naive. Unfortunately, extending trust to someone who doesn't deserve it is very common. You can read more about this issue in my book *Love Secrets Revealed* (2006).

Here's what causes the problem: we feel compelled to trust someone we care about. When you love someone, shouldn't you trust that person? We wouldn't even think about being in a committed relationship with someone we didn't trust, would we? Believing we are obligated to trust someone we care about is a myth perpetuated in our culture.

You've heard the expression that *love is blind*. I've also heard it said that *marriage is the institution for the blind*. The truth is that most people are not worthy of trust. I'm not trying to be cynical; I am being realistic. It isn't all bad news, however. We all have the potential to become trustworthy, but it takes work—hard work—and the ability to be honest with ourselves to see where we are not worthy of trust.

Our emotional dependency doesn't want to face the reality that someone we love may not be trustworthy. So we betray ourselves by believing they are worthy of trust, when they are not. Our wishful thinking makes us see our partners as we *want* them to be, not as they *are*. We go on living with the fantasy of who they are until they do something that shatters our world and forces us to see reality. *We cannot be betrayed without some form of self-betrayal also operating behind the scenes.*

There is another dimension to this issue that needs to be explored. We also have trouble admitting it when *we* are not trustworthy. If you are early in recovery, you know what I mean: if you've been at it for a while, just think back to those early days when we all wondered, "How can someone trust us if we cannot trust ourselves?"

Our desire to manipulate and control how people feel about us compels us to deceive them and mask the truth that we are unworthy of trust. So we try to convince our loved ones that we are trustworthy when we aren't. We feel compelled to trust, and expect to be trusted, without working on building trust.

There is something powerful operating here that we need to talk more about. Our society has fused love and dependency. We mistakenly believe that when someone loves you, they will take care of you. Our culture has legitimized emotional dependency as a reasonable expectation of love. If you love me, you will make me feel safe. If you love me, you will do what I want you to do, you won't hurt me, and you will know what I want before I ask. It's all nonsense! This is a fantasy of how love is supposed to be, but it is not true. It's not mature love; it is immature love.

Mature love promotes autonomy and authenticity, not obligation and dependency. Mature love encourages individuality, not conformity. It is rooted in taking responsibility for ourselves and our feelings. Mature love balances our needs for togetherness and individuality, while respecting differences and encouraging honesty. Mature love faces the reality of who two people are and who they aren't.

So here's the point of this discussion that is most relevant for making amends: we know that people extended trust to us when they shouldn't have. We mapped their minds and figured out their weaknesses. Whether we did this consciously or not is irrelevant. The point is that we knew how to manipulate them and we used this knowledge to our advantage. We played them like a master violinist plays a violin. This is one of the things we realized when we made our list of those we harmed and explored what we did to harm them. We became the puppeteer and they were our puppets. We didn't care what we were doing to them—all that mattered is what we wanted.

We read their desires and intentions and used the information we obtained to get them to stay connected to us. That way we could continue manipulating them to support our addiction or to cave in to our unreasonable emotional demands. If they had a fear of abandonment, we used that fear to maneuver them to put up with our inappropriate or abusive behavior. If they were anxious, we used their anxiety to manipulate their perception of reality. If they were insecure, we fed their insecurity by telling them that no one would ever want them, which really meant that they were stuck putting up with our rotten behavior or they were going to end up alone. We convinced them that right was wrong, and wrong was right. It's tough to admit we did this. We don't like to think of ourselves as evil, but there is a part of us that is.

It is no wonder that no one could trust us: we weren't trust-worthy! Who can trust us if we are Machiavellian, or if we are only concerned with winning at any cost? Who can trust us when we ignore our personal ethics or values? Who can trust us when we treat others as sources for our gratification? We *can't* be trusted when we are operating out of this part of our psyche!

When this evil or reptilian part of us ran the show, we got a kind of sick pride from feeling superior to others, by being able to either intimidate them, outthink them, or outmaneuver them. We felt a false-pride from our ability to control and manipulate people, places, and things. This part of us felt like it was our right to treat people like objects. It's hard to be honest about this because it's very primitive behavior that no one likes to admit or own.

Remember what I shared with you about my wanting to win but being ashamed that I was found out? I wanted to manipulate my friend Bill, but I didn't want him to realize he was being manipulated. I knew that using him to feel better about myself was wrong. It felt wrong, and that's why I was ashamed about being exposed, but I manipulated him anyway. My need for superiority was more important than our friendship—it didn't matter to me that it was wrong. What a lousy friend I was to Bill. We must all see this difficult truth about ourselves if we are going to be worthy of trust.

Being trustworthy is sacred. It requires that we operate from the best in us, not the worst in us. This is a very important hidden reward from working Steps 8, 9, and 10. We restore trust in our relationships because we are worthy of being trusted. This does not mean that we become perfect and therefore won't ever do wrong again. We strive for progress, not perfection. We will never be perfect. We will, at times, let the worst in us run the show. But if we commit ourselves to accurate self-appraisal, we will recognize when we are wrong and clean it up. When we allow the best in us to be in charge, we will feel pride in being humble, in being just, in being able to face our worst behavior, in admitting when we are wrong, and in learning from our experience. We are human *beings*. When we function from the best in us, we will be worthy of trust and enjoy the confidence others can have in our integrity. What an amazing gift these three Steps give us.

Hidden Reward 7:
Being of Value

We have taken corrective actions to be the person we'd like to be, which has helped us feel better about ourselves. Working Steps 8, 9, and 10 helps us develop a more positive self-concept, which we need because our self-concept was quite poor. We have often been described as egomaniacs who suffer from an inferiority complex; despite our bravado, we haven't felt worthy of success or love. How could we be OK with ourselves when we had no regard for the well-being of others? We used and abused the people in our lives to fulfill our needs, without any concern for what we were doing to them. We left a wake of destruction behind us with our self-will running riot.

I recall watching video of the terrible tsunami that hit the coast of Japan in early 2011. As it rolled across the land, it devoured everything that lay in its path. Its destructive power was mind-boggling, toppling buildings like they were constructed from balsa wood. It tossed cars and trucks around like they were toys and ripped trees from the ground like they had no roots.

I had a thought while watching the tsunami that it was like watching a person's addiction destroy everything important to them. Our addiction leaves a terrible wake of destruction in its path, including shattered dreams, shattered trust, betrayal, pain, disappointment, and suffering. It's as if we were cursed with a spell that was the opposite of the Midas touch: everything we touched turned to dust, not gold.

Working the Twelve Steps helps us stop the juggernaut of destruction that was released by our false-self and addiction. While the Steps helped stop these destructive forces, they also released other positive forces, such as our desire to be of value to another person. This desire was always a part of who we were, but it lay dormant in our souls: there was no room for this desire to be expressed under the rule of the false-self and addict-self. By cleaning house, we cleared enough space for this desire to have a place in our lives. This is another one of the hidden rewards in working Steps 8, 9, and 10.

We want to be a positive force in our lives and in the lives of others. This desire has become increasingly more important to us. We enjoy a new purpose in our lives: to be of value to the person who is still suffering from addiction. But this desire extends far beyond helping only those who still suffer from this disease. We want to make a positive difference in our families, in our communities, and in our world. We want to become a true citizen who makes his or her community a better place to live.

Dr. Viktor Frankl, a brilliant psychiatrist who was imprisoned in a concentration camp in World War II, believed that self-actualization was only possible through self-transcendence. In other words, we have to get out of ourselves to actualize our human potential. We have to give ourselves to a cause that is much greater than we are. We need to be of value to realize our full human potential.

Dr. Frankl described the process this way: "... true meaning of life is to be discovered in the world rather than within man or his own psyche." He called this "the self-transcendence of human existence" (1984, 115). We transcend our existence through service, through being of value to a cause or to another person who is suffering. Dr. Frankl noted that "the more one forgets himself—by giving himself to a cause to serve or another person to love—the more human he is and the more he actualizes himself" (115).

A major shift in our thinking has taken place through working Steps 8, 9, and 10. Before, it was all about us. We were self-centered and self-absorbed. Now we are concerned with being of value, with restoring trust, with making whole those we have harmed. We sincerely want to make a difference and help someone who is still suffering. We have turned a weakness into a strength. We have turned our wounds into something sacred that helps others and restores social justice. We've come a long way, baby!

I have been working recently with an elderly woman who was addicted to Vicodin. She has worked hard in her recovery and recently started making amends, even going so far as to visit the urgent care centers where she frequently went to get her Vicodin. She told the doctor on duty that the purpose of her visit was to make amends for manipulating the doctors on duty, and misusing their time when they could have been seeing a patient who really needed their expertise. She offered to be on call if they ever had a patient who might profit from talking to her.

She also made amends to all of her adult children, and to her husband. She was on a roll. Her self-concept was improving. When we first met two years ago, she had compulsively apologized for everything. It seemed like she was apologizing for taking up the space she occupied and even for the oxygen she breathed. Eventually she stopped apologizing, except when upon self-appraisal she realized she was wrong. About three months ago, we discussed that it might be time to sponsor a newcomer. Her first response was to minimize her experience, which was consistent with her self-effacing attitude. She doubted that she had anything to offer a newcomer.

I challenged her self-effacing response, and she quickly saw how she was using it as a way of avoiding the anxiety that working with a newcomer would provoke. She was concerned that she'd say the wrong thing and mess up their recovery or that she would misdirect them and they'd relapse. I told her that she wasn't that powerful. This was her catastrophic thinking, which had always controlled her life and stopped her from taking risks. She realized the truth in this feedback and agreed to put the word out to the fellowship that she was available for sponsorship.

I saw her two months later. She had started working with a young woman who was also addicted to opioids and Xanax. She glowed as she discussed how she was spending time with this newcomer and walking her through the First Step. She was moved by how satisfying it was to her soul to be of service. It felt so gratifying that she decided to volunteer at a women's treatment program, where she led a discussion group on the Twelve Steps. We did a lot of good work together, but the positive effect I've seen in her self-concept from working with others could never be created within the four walls of my office.

Hidden Reward 8:
Learning to Self-Soothe and Regulate Our Emotions

Because of our inability to support ourselves and stand on our own two feet, we manipulated others to satisfy our needs. Steps 8, 9, and 10 teach us how to support ourselves and take care of our needs while simultaneously maintaining a healthy and respectful connection to others. We can only grow up if we stop manipulating others to take care of our needs and learn how to support ourselves as we flow with the cycle of experience, the ups and downs and in-betweens of life.

Our energy for growth was misdirected at manipulating others to make us feel OK rather than tapping into the internal resources we have that would maintain our sense of well-being. We forgot how to soothe ourselves and regulate our emotions because we were so focused on getting someone else to do it for us. Self-soothing is programmed into us. We see evidence of this in infants, who instinctively soothe themselves. They will cry and fuss, but eventually calm down and fall asleep. We have it too, but unfortunately we haven't trusted ourselves enough to realize it.

Instead of following the cycle of our experience, which would automatically lead us to self-soothe and take care of our needs, we fine-tuned our abilities to manipulate our environment to satisfy our needs. We became emotionally dependent on others to comfort us, to make us feel safe, to soothe our anxiety and fears, or to satisfy our needs.

We fused our emotional well-being to other people's words and deeds, which made them far too important. Needless to say, we became highly reactive to their moods, their behavior, or their emotions. We ended up taking their thoughts and actions personally. We believed that their behavior toward us determined our self-worth. This is what drove us to manipulate them—we regulated their behavior because they regulated us. We manipulated them because we didn't want to feel controlled by them.

Dr. Fritz Perls, a brilliant therapist and a major force in humanistic psychology, believed that our manipulations are always directed at preserving and cherishing our handicap rather than getting rid of it. This is why we kept trying to get support and validation from our environment: deep down, we didn't think we could support and comfort ourselves. Our manipulation reinforced the idea that we couldn't cope with our pain and anxiety. We reinforced a concept of ourselves as incapable, inadequate, and inferior. We cannot grow up if we choose to continue to control and manipulate our environment, and seek external validation. We have to challenge this old idea, or our recovery will never be fully realized.

This means that becoming self-supportive is critical to peace of mind, which raises the question, "What does it mean to be self-supportive?" Being self-supportive begins with the attitude that we are responsible for our lives, well-being, and actions in all the areas that are open to our choices (Branden 1996). This means that we are responsible for our emotional well-being as well as how we respond to our emotions.

Steps 8, 9, and 10 help us step up and become responsible for our lives, our emotional well-being, and our actions like never before. Here are a few of the ways we change as a result:

- We take responsibility for the level of awareness we bring to our lives.
- We don't blame others for what we have done wrong.
- We practice accurate self-appraisal to ensure that we promptly admit when we are wrong to keep our egos in check, and to keep our emotions balanced and modulated.
- We keep our side of the street clean while aiming at being our best self.
- We pray and meditate to soothe ourselves, comfort ourselves, and regulate our emotions.
- We ask for help when we are overwhelmed, frustrated, frightened, resentful, anxious, or lost.
- We take total responsibility for our actions and for generating the causes of the effects we want. (Branden 1996, 92)

We know that when the wrong part of us is in charge, we will lose control and—more often than not—hurt others. When our raging and destructive Mr. Hyde surfaces, no one is safe.

Soothing ourselves and regulating our emotions involves being honest with ourselves about who we are. If we are unreasonable but don't see it, we will continue to demand obedience. If we are manipulative but don't face it, we will continue to try to play games.

Honesty—rigorous honesty—with ourselves and others becomes the antidote to becoming the raging Mr. Hyde. The more honest we are with ourselves and others, the more the best in us is running the show. When the best in us runs the show, we can invent what we need to do to regulate emotions like anxiety and fear.

Here is the thing that is often overlooked by many psycho-therapists: *Soothing ourselves isn't something that we need to learn. We already know how to soothe ourselves.*

Right now you may be thinking, "Dr. Berger, have I heard you right? I don't need to learn how to soothe myself? That's not what my therapist tells me." Yes, this is what I said, and I will tell you why.

Soothing ourselves is hardwired into our physiology. It is part of the homeostatic mechanism we are all born with if we are neuro-logically intact, that is to say, if our brains are healthy and normal at birth. If the ability to soothe ourselves were not innate, we wouldn't have survived as a species. This mechanism helped us calm ourselves, relax, lick our wounds, regroup, and reenergize. If our ancestors hadn't been able to recharge this way, they would have burned out trying to stay alive, and the same is true for us today. The impor-tant question is, if we are born with this ability, what happened that interfered with it? Why can't we comfort ourselves?

As I discussed earlier, we naturally invent what we need to do to satisfy our needs, *so long as we don't interfere with the cycle of experi-ence.* The trouble is that most of the time the rules of our false-self override the cycle of experience. In the process, we forget our capac-ity to self-soothe. Here's an example of how this happened in my personal life.

My father passed away from multiple myeloma, a type of blood cancer, when I was eleven years old. He died on December 26, 1963. After receiving the call from the hospital that my mother, Louise Berger, anticipated, she came into the living room, where I was play-ing with my younger sister and younger brother. She sobbed as she told us the news, that our father had died early that morning. I went into shock. I froze inside. I had lost the most important man in my life that day.

I loved my dad. He was a great father. On the weekends, we would often visit one of the great museums in Chicago, such as the Museum of Natural History. When we entered the museum, we'd stop in the main hall that led to the various exhibits and look at the two wonderful dinosaurs displayed. There stood a T-rex and a triceratops facing off for battle. The scene was magnificent. My dad would tell us a story about the battle that was taking place between the two dinosaurs. Sometimes the T-rex would win and have a feast, and other times the triceratops would pierce the aggressive T-rex with one of its sharp horns and drive the beast off. I lived for these moments. Alvin Jerome Berger loved teaching us about the world, and I loved listening to him.

When he passed away I was devastated, but I wouldn't allow myself to grieve his loss. I interfered with the cycle of experience. If I had followed my experience, I would have dropped to the floor and sobbed. Instead, I froze my feelings that day. I didn't want to feel that pain; I was afraid to feel that much pain. So I avoided my feelings by shutting myself down. The following weekend I was sitting in the lobby of the funeral home reading a Spider-Man comic as the rabbi chanted next to my father's coffin in the other room.

I lost a part of myself, an important part of myself, when my father died. I cut myself off from caring, from feeling, from needing anyone. I never wanted to hurt or be disappointed again. My false-self decided that I had to be needless and wantless to be OK. About six months later, a friend of mine offered me a cold beer. I drank it, and I loved it. I felt alive. I don't know if I was born an alcoholic, but the minute I drank that beer on that hot summer day, an alcoholic was born. That was in 1964. Seven years later, I returned from Vietnam with a full-blown drug addiction. As I described earlier, serendipity helped me get treatment for my drug problem at my final duty station at the Kaneohe Marine Corps Air Station. After about sixty days of being clean and sober, my friend Bill and I signed up for a weekend group therapy session for personal growth held in Honolulu near the University of Hawaii. It was facilitated by two therapists from the university, a man and a woman. One of the leaders, Sasha, was an anthropologist and a very well-trained personal growth facilitator. He started the group with a guided imagery exercise. He asked us to close our eyes and imagine someone we needed to say good-bye to. Of course, my father came to mind immediately.

Sasha had each of us go around the group and discuss who came to mind. When my turn came around, he must have sensed the massive grief that was pressed deep down in my soul. He asked me if I'd be willing to talk to my father and say good-bye to him. I innocently and naively agreed. He put a pillow in front of me and said, "Here's your father. Say good-bye to him."

What happened next saved my life! The dam broke inside of me. I thawed out. I started sobbing, telling my father how much I missed him and needed him. I yelled at God for prematurely taking my father away from me and my family. I yelled at my dad for not being there. Fully engaged and present, I was following my experience, trusting that my experiences were making me feel exactly what I needed to feel, helping me say exactly what needed to be said. It was an unbelievably powerful experience.

I was amazed at how deeply I felt about his loss. I had cut myself off from my grief, from my real-self, but it was in this group that I started to recover my true-self. After about three hours of releasing these repressed feelings, I was blown away by how pure and purged I felt. I finally felt comfortable in my own skin, and my visual and auditory acuity was off the charts.

I had experienced these keen sensations before, when I had

dropped acid during my active addiction. LSD created an acute sensory experience: Everything vibrated. Everything looked bright and alive. My consciousness seemed to expand and become one with the universe.

Self-soothing—which is what my tears and grief were—was deeper than the "best" acid trip I'd ever had. After I had grieved my grief, cried my tears, screamed my outrage, and protested the injustice, I opened my eyes and felt more connected and alive than ever in my life, even more connected than I felt on acid. But this experience was organic and natural. It was the result of following my experience and letting it guide me. It was the result of letting go and not letting all the nonsense I told myself prevent me from expressing my true feelings.

I felt a degree of self-soothing that I had never before experienced as an adult. My voice changed that night, my throat relaxed, my stomach relaxed—my soul relaxed.

Crying, shouting, sobbing, trembling, dancing, screaming, hitting, kicking, biting, tearing, and stomping, along with honesty, authenticity, making amends, and accurate self-appraisal are some of the homeostatic mechanisms we have to soothe our pain.

When our false-self dictated that crying was wrong, we would stop ourselves from crying. We'd stop ourselves from crying by choking off our pain. The muscles in our neck would tighten in a certain way to stop the emotion from surfacing. We'd interrupt the cycle of experience. This blocking prevented us from following our experience.

As my experience in group therapy shows, we can work through our resistance in order to experience our reality and soothe ourselves.

Steps 8, 9, and 10 do the same thing that happened to me that day when I faced my grief. They promote our awareness of what we have done wrong by forcing us to face our pain. We sit with the reality of our behavior, which creates compassion and motivates us to take action to right our wrongs and restore the wholeness of our victims. We flow through the cycle of experience and begin to resolve our unfinished business.

Resolving unfinished business releases the psychic energy that was bonded to the unfinished business, and that energy then becomes available to help us cope with what is happening right now in our lives. This is another hidden reward of working these Steps. Now let's turn our attention to how Steps 8, 9, and 10 improve our self-concept.

Hidden Reward 9:
Better Self-Esteem and a More Positive Self-Concept

As we have seen, Steps 8 through 10 focus on how our false-self has wreaked havoc on our relationships. In this chapter, I want to help you understand how working these Steps helps improve your self-concept and raise your self-esteem. This is another hidden reward that is the result of working these challenging Steps.

Because our need for connection to others is so profound, nothing triggers our "issues" (insecurity, jealousy, anger, mistrust) as powerfully as a relationship does. Ironically, as a relationship becomes more important and intimate, we find it more difficult to hold on to ourselves. We become overly sensitive to what our partner is or isn't doing because our self-esteem is determined by how they feel about us.

The more emotionally differentiated we are, the more our self-esteem will be independent of our partner's feelings or behavior, and the better we will balance our individuality with the pressure we feel for togetherness. If we are not well differentiated, we will lose ourselves in the connection. Our self-esteem will be fragile and unstable. We will make other people too important and allow them to define us. We react to this emotional fusion by either moving against them (controlling or rebelling), moving away from them (emotionally withdrawing), or moving toward them (people pleasing). If we are not well differentiated, our self-esteem will be dependent on our partner's behavior and the connection will control us.

The difficult truth to face is that we save our worst behavior for those we love. Our relationships bring out the best in us as well as the worst in us. Relationships are "people growers," according to Drs. David Schnarch and Walter Kempler (Schnarch 2009; Kempler 1982). They can be our best teachers if we genuinely want to learn about who we see ourselves to be (our self-concept) and how we feel about ourselves (our self-esteem). For instance, if we view ourselves as someone who is *unlovable,* we sabotage the efforts of others to love us by demanding that they *prove* to us that we are lovable. Another way of protecting ourselves may be to reject them before they reject us because we believe their rejection is inevitable; after all, we are unlovable. Or, we may run away at the first sign that someone may be interested in us because we don't want to risk being rejected.

If we have no respect for ourselves (and are filled with guilt and shame), we will defy the efforts of others to show us consideration and respect. This is where our sense of self-worth (a key component of self-esteem) is so important. When we see ourselves as unworthy of happiness in relationships, we will make our partner miserable if they make the mistake of trying to love us. But the way to address this issue is not simply through affirmations of "I am a lovable, worthwhile person." Repeating affirmations may help, but the deeper and more helpful path is to become aware of, acknowledge, and open up our feelings of unworthiness, while doing esteem-able acts like making amends or promptly admitting when we are wrong.

Just as admitting our addictions opens the door to healing, admitting our darkest feelings of unworthiness, shame, guilt, and fear allows these feelings to change as well.

Could it be possible that who we are is good enough? Is it true that we don't have to be perfect to belong and to be loved and accepted? The answer is yes. This is what the famous psychologist Carl Rogers (1961) found in his clinical work. When his clients faced who they were openly, being good enough was no longer an issue. It was irrelevant. But as you can see, this is at the heart of our problem. Because we have let our false-self impose rules on us that are impossible to satisfy, we end up feeling like we are not good enough. We lack the support of our own self-esteem, which makes us dependent on our environment to support us and validate us. Steps 8 through 10 help us become more self-supporting through our own contributions. We detach our self-esteem from others and reattach it to ourselves. We grow up and stand on our own two feet. We root our self-esteem in doing the right thing because it is the right thing to do, not because it is going to get us external validation or support.

Can you see the wisdom in the tradition that encourages us to place principles before personality? This guideline encourages us to stop reacting and instead center ourselves in a more thoughtful and mindful practice. It encourages us to listen to the best in ourselves.

By learning incredibly valuable information in Steps 8 through 10 about our destructive and hurtful relationship behavior, we become able to change that behavior. The pain of our past can then have value, becoming our teacher.

When we work Step 8, we deal our false-self, our ego, a major blow. When we begin facing the truth of how many people we have harmed, and the many ways we harmed them, the reality of the pain we have caused can stop us in our tracks. We will be humbled— deeply humbled. Our false-pride, arrogance, defensiveness, and need to look good will be challenged in a profound way. We will see that we can handle the truth about our behavior in relationships. We can even learn that once we commit to facing painful truths about our treatment of others and make amends, much of the weight of our shame and guilt can be lifted from us. Once again, we learn that our pain can illuminate a path to liberation.

For those of you who have worked Step 8, think about the effect that doing so has had in your life. Many of us find that we begin to feel better about ourselves as we get more honest about who we are and whom we have hurt. In identifying with our false-self and living with the effects of addiction, we lost most, if not all, of our self-respect and sense of our own worth and value.

By identifying those we have harmed and taking responsibility for the damage we have done, we begin to create genuine self-respect and self-worth within ourselves. We are doing something that is difficult and takes courage. This builds our self-esteem and helps us see ourselves more positively.

As we work Step 9 and make amends to those we have harmed, our self-respect continues to grow. We begin to be someone we can admire in our relationships. We're building something real and solid within ourselves, and with others. We are becoming our true-self. Instead of living a life based on manipulating others with lies and other dishonest tricks to feel OK, we start to build a life based on truth and honesty. We begin to have real relationships based on authenticity.

Practicing Step 10 keeps us humble and protects us from the worst in ourselves. This Step helps us deal better with conflict because we don't have to convince anyone that we are right and they are wrong. Let's face it: no one likes to be made to feel wrong.

We start learning to balance our deep desire to cooperate with others with our simultaneous need to maintain our integrity. Our true-self needs both. We also become more aware of our emotional dependency, and all the ways we sell out our souls to hold on to another person's love. (There is a more detailed discussion of this process in *12 Smart Things to Do When the Booze and Drugs Are Gone*.)

Feeling better about who we are as we treat ourselves and others with more respect and compassion is what we call *self-esteem*. Self-esteem theorist and therapist Nathaniel Branden (1994) defines self-esteem as "the disposition to experience oneself as competent to cope with the basic challenges of life and as worthy of happiness" (27).

What he means by this is that there are two fundamental parts to our self-esteem. One is our *self-confidence:* Can I cope with the demands of life? Can I cope with recovery? Can I support myself financially, emotionally, and spiritually? Can I maintain healthy relationships? Do I feel confident in my ability to learn and grow psychologically and spiritually? Can I step up and work the Steps?

The other fundamental piece of self-esteem is *self-worth:* Do I have a sense of my own worth and value? Do I feel worthy of happiness, love, and success? Do I like how I function in my relationships? Am I willing to honor my true-self consistently in my life, especially when it's hard to do so?

Dr. Branden also thought about self-esteem as the reputation we acquire with ourselves. How is your reputation with yourself? Would you want to be friends with or be married to someone like you? Can you look yourself in the eye and feel good about how you treat your family and friends? Are you proud of yourself for who you are?

Steps 8 through 10 help us improve our reputation with ourselves. We carry our guilt, shame, grief, and fear for years and sometimes decades, until we bring them to the light of consciousness and face them. No one can force us to acknowledge the harm we've done to others: we must choose to do so. And it is in making this choice that real self-esteem begins and our reputation with ourselves improves.

We are born with intrinsic worth and value. We have value and worth not because of the possessions we acquire or the power we have attained, but simply because we are here, and we are alive. *Our be-ing has innate worth.* And yet, our self-esteem is also raised and strengthened, is *earned,* through the choices we make and the actions we take. This is a powerful principle: *Whenever we choose to face and deal with a difficult and painful truth about ourselves, and take positive action, we improve our self-esteem.* This is precisely what happens as a result of the work we do in Steps 8 and 9. We step up and face the worst in us, and then take action to restore social justice by making whole those we hurt. This raises our self-esteem and helps us reconstruct a more positive self-concept.

Whenever we choose to avoid and run from reality, we diminish our self-esteem. But whenever we honor our true-self, while simultaneously respecting (and even encouraging) the need of others to honor *their* true-self, our self-esteem grows stronger and our self-concept becomes more positive.

When we choose to see ourselves more realistically, warts and all, we become better at accepting ourselves as we are. As this happens, we become more able to accept others as they are. A practice that promotes self-awareness is central to self-esteem and recovery.

Self-awareness, responsibility, and self-reflection create the foundation for our new self-concept. These are the building blocks for our self-esteem. But as we make progress in our recovery, other elements of self-esteem can be strengthened within us, such as self-assertiveness, living with integrity, and living with a purpose (Branden 1994). One way of looking at the therapeutic effect of the Twelve Steps is that they reconstruct our understanding of ourselves by creating a more positive self-concept and by improving our self-esteem. We experience a major psychic shift that supports and sustains our recovery efforts and encourages us to have better relationships with our fellows.

When I first met Jose he could hardly look me in the eye. He was nine months sober, but his sobriety was on shaky ground. Jose hated his life. He was terribly shy and socially awkward. Not surprisingly, when Jose drank, he became a lot more comfortable. The social anxiety dissipated and he could act like he was confident and socially competent.

When he was sober, it was a totally different story. This is what motivated Jose to come and seek my help. He told me that he suffered from a deep sense of hopelessness and loneliness. He didn't think he would ever find a way to be comfortable in AA meetings, ever be able to find a partner, or ever have the kind of life he dreamed about. He was pessimistic and resigned to living out a miserable life. His self-esteem was at rock bottom.

As we talked, I realized that one of the things that was creating Jose's self-consciousness was his belief that other people harshly judged him. Often the feelings that we imagine other people have about us are based on the projection of our low self-esteem. So I asked Jose if he'd be willing to try an experiment. He agreed.

I pulled up an empty chair, placed it in front of Jose, and said, "I want you to imagine that you are sitting in front of Jose. You are in the other chair. The chair you are sitting in represents all the people who judge you. Do you understand?" He nodded.

"What do you want me to do?" he asked.

I told him that I wanted him to judge Jose. "I want you to give a voice to all the things you imagine people are thinking about you."

Here's what happened:

People judging Jose: You are a frightened little boy. You have screwed up your life, your drinking has ruined everything, and because of that you can't even drink to feel comfortable. You don't know how to have friends or even talk to a woman you are interested in without worrying about embarrassing yourself or saying something stupid. No one will ever want to be with you. You will never succeed in life. You are a loser.

Jose (after I told him to change chairs and answer for himself): You are right. I am a loser. No one will ever love me. I am hopeless. Just leave me alone and let me die.

People judging Jose: Even your response is pitiful. When are you going to get a backbone? You are a loser.

Jose: I don't know what to say. He's right—I am hopeless. I am a loser.

It was quite obvious that as Jose did this shuttle technique, what he was really experiencing was a projection of his poor self-esteem. I stopped him and said, "The problem is not what other people are thinking about you. It's what you are thinking about yourself. Your reputation with yourself stinks." I didn't see Jose as "helpless" or a "loser." This is how Jose feels about himself; he projected his low self-esteem onto the world. He believed that other people felt the same way toward him that he felt about himself, and he lost the ability to see himself as a whole person—as a human *being*. He identified with his despised-self and didn't yet see his possible self.

Had I taken the traditional approach to therapy and given Jose some self-affirmations to help him raise his self-esteem, it wouldn't have helped. He needed to empower himself and raise his self-esteem by working Steps 8 and 9. He needed to get acquainted with the parts of himself that existed in his blind spot. I encouraged him to contact his sponsor and get to work on making amends.

Jose was willing. He was sick and tired of being sick and tired. He called his sponsor after leaving the session and set up a time for them to meet and begin discussing Step 8.

Four months later, Jose came back to see me. He had been working hard at making amends to the people and institutions he had harmed. It was tough going, but the results were obvious. He looked me in the eye for the entire session, confident and proud of himself for stepping up and making amends. He recounted several very difficult amends that he had made, especially the ones to his brother and sister. He had betrayed them on numerous occasions, and they were suspicious of his motivation to make amends. They didn't trust him, but Jose was OK with this. He didn't judge them or resent them for their suspiciousness; he understood that he had created this problem, and he didn't let it subtract from or redefine his efforts at cleaning up his side of the street. He stood on his own two feet and made amends for his lies, schemes, deceptions, and manipulations. He took total responsibility for what he had done wrong. He felt empowered.

In the months that followed, we worked on dealing with the trauma he felt from having a critical and abusive father. There were many very painful and tearful moments in these sessions as he dealt with his own emotional wounds, as well as those he had inflicted on others. Today, Jose is happily married and has celebrated over ten years of sobriety. He rarely experiences the social anxiety that so plagued him in early recovery.

Jose's recovery illustrates an important point that I want to take a moment and discuss. Many of us feel depressed and anxious when we enter recovery because of who we have become and how we have lived our lives. Diagnosing these feelings as the real cause of our troubles is putting the cart before the horse. It's like blaming the swelling on a broken arm for the broken bone. Feeling depressed and anxious is the result of letting the worst in us run the show. Feeling bad for hurting others, being selfish, and destroying everything that lay in our path means that something is right about us, not wrong. I'd be worried if someone in the early phases of recovery felt *good* about themselves.

We don't need to treat these painful and disturbing feelings as though they are our primary problem. It is best if we can use the pain and discomfort these feelings cause to motivate us toward corrective action: to go to meetings and work the Steps, to get a sponsor, to get honest with ourselves and face our problems—use them as motivation to take the necessary steps toward reconstructing our self-concept and discovering our true potential.

Steps 8, 9, and 10 have given us the hidden reward of developing a more positive self-concept that is based on reality—the reality of who we are and what we are doing. This is a much more accurate view of ourselves because it is based on who we are and what we are doing rather than on an idealized image of who we should be and how we should act.

Our self-esteem has improved. We are more capable of dealing with the world on its terms, and we feel more worthy of success and love. Our new self is more solid, resilient, and flexible. It is less dependent on the limited perceptions of others for validation. We have reached a degree of autonomy in our connections with others. We are well on the road to recovering our true-self.

The next hidden reward is essential to true peace of mind and serenity. As you are about to see, restoring our integrity is critical to letting the best in us operate the rest of us.

Hidden Reward 10:
Integrity

Let us start by defining *integrity*. This word is often used synonymously with *honesty* and *authenticity*. If someone is thought to be authentic or honest, they are also thought to possess integrity. This is partially true, but it still doesn't capture the full nature of this important characteristic. Although authenticity and honesty are necessary to achieve integrity, integrity encompasses more than these two traits.

To achieve integrity, we must adopt a disciplined practice of rigorous honesty, self-evaluation, and authenticity. These are the tools we refine or develop by working Steps 8, 9, and 10. Now we are going to see that they also help us become more integrated. Let us explore the concept of integrity.

Integrity serves a very important function in our lives. It is like the glue that holds us together: it connects or bonds the different parts of ourselves so they can work together in a harmonious and coordinated effort. Dr. Nathaniel Branden, the gifted therapist and self-esteem expert, defined integrity as incorporating our convictions, our standards, our values, and our beliefs into the way we behave. He went on to say that "integrity is loyalty in action to the judgment of our consciousness" (1985, 212). Dr. Branden's insight into integrity helps us see the critical role that making amends plays in the development of our integrity. It is through making amends that we demonstrate a loyalty in action to our real-self.

But the Steps help us integrate other parts of ourselves too. In order to integrate our convictions, our values, and our beliefs into our behavior we must bring into harmony the warring factions in our personalities. We must find a way to use our awareness to resolve the conflict and create a state of cooperation. Let me explain the importance of integrating these disparate parts of ourselves.

When we split ourselves into the "good-self" and the "bad-self," energy becomes frozen and unavailable for our use. Miriam and Erving Polster, two brilliant Gestalt therapists, observed: "In the uneasy alignment that the individual achieved between two opposed qualities in himself, one part of his nature was disarmed of its excitement and activity" (1973, 67). When we polarize two parts of ourselves, we become inflexible. We no longer have the full range of possibilities that exist along the continuum of these two poles. Our false-self makes one side of the continuum right or OK and the other side wrong and undesirable.

To understand this better, let's use Philip's experience as an example. Philip decided that to be liked and accepted, he must always be Mr. Nice Guy. He split himself into the good-self, Mr. Nice Guy, and the rejected bad-self, Mr. Hyde. Whenever the undesirable side of his personality surfaced—his Mr. Hyde, so to speak—he became anxious and employed face-saving measures to erase any evidence of Mr. Hyde from his consciousness.

He would disown Mr. Hyde by projecting him onto the world

or blame Mr. Hyde's appearance on someone else's behavior. Philip's Mr. Nice Guy wouldn't ever act this way, now, would he? Well, yes, he would, because his Mr. Nice Guy isn't just a nice guy either; there is more to him than that. He is also Mr. Hyde and many other selves. He is, in fact, a population of different selves, as we all are.

When Philip split himself off from Mr. Hyde, the energy from this part of Philip was no longer available for use. It was frozen in Mr. Hyde. With help, Philip renewed the contact between these two aspects of himself and integrated them into his personality. When Philip integrated Mr. Nice Guy and Mr. Hyde, their natures changed through the effect of one upon the other. When appropriate, Philip could be a real nice guy, but when necessary he could also be appropriately assertive and hold on to himself. By integrating these two parts of himself, Philip came one step closer to becoming his true-self.

This integration occurred because Philip learned to suspend the erroneous belief that these two parts were incompatible. They were not, and neither were any of the other warring factions within him. They *seemed* incompatible because they didn't fit Philip's idealized image of himself—Mr. Hyde was not considered valid by his false-self. But, in reality, these two parts were not incompatible.

We are fragmented too. Change the names of the two opposing characters to fit your own situation. The Hero vs. The Coward? Mrs. Healthy vs. Ms. Unhealthy? The Intelligent One vs. The Stupid One? The Good One vs. The Bad One? The Addict vs. The Healthy Self? The list could go on and on and on. The point is, we all have many conflicted parts of ourselves. The healthier we become, the less conflict we have between the various parts of ourselves. The less conflict we have, the greater our peace of mind. This is what it means to be comfortable in our own skin. We work *with* ourselves, not *against* ourselves. We support ourselves, rather than sabotage ourselves. We respond from all of us, not just the part of us that we think is acceptable. We act as a whole person. We act with integrity.

Working Steps 8, 9, and 10 brings us face-to-face with the conflicts that exist between the various incompatible parts of ourselves. By making a list of those we harmed, by being willing to make amends to them all, by making amends, and by practicing accurate self-evaluation, we resolve the conflict between our false-self and our real-self—between the part of us that justifies our rotten behavior and the part of us that wants to restore justice. We integrate the part of us that wants to be right with the part of us that has compassion. We integrate our basic need for togetherness and cooperation with our basic need to be ourselves and hold on to our individuality. We put Humpty Dumpty back together again. We restore our integrity. We restore our wholeness.

Integrity is never painless. We have to let the parts of us that are in conflict rub up against each other; we have to fully experience the tension of conflicting demands, interests, or desires and be willing to be emotionally torn apart in the process. It is through this tension that integration occurs.

We need all of the parts of ourselves that we once thought were incompatible to work together and provide support for our efforts in recovery, specifically during the challenging and difficult tasks inherent in these three Steps. Unresolved conflicts between these various parts of ourselves will undermine our efforts in recovery, and will result in anxiety and depression. We can't have a part of us wanting to make amends and another part of us resisting that effort. When we find harmony between these warring parts of ourselves, we will know peace of mind and serenity. We will be comfortable in our own skin. The best in us will be able to use all the rest of us to appropriately satisfy our needs.

Integration is ongoing, as Dr. Fritz Perls reminded us:

There is not such a thing as total integration. Integration is never completed, maturation is never completed. It's an ongoing process for ever and ever. . . . There's always something to be integrated; always something to be learned. There's always a possibility of richer maturation —of taking more and more responsibility for yourself and for your life. (1969, 64–65)

This is why we say that recovery is a *process,* not an event. There is always something to learn in recovery, always a lesson to integrate, always a next step in our emotional maturation and development. This is the purpose of Step 10. It promotes self-awareness and responsibility. It promotes taking more and more responsibility for ourselves and our lives.

The restoration of our integrity is another hidden reward of working Steps 8, 9, and 10.

Hidden Reward 11:
Intimacy: "I to Thou"
Connections

Martin Buber, a brilliant philosophy professor at Hebrew University in Jerusalem, was the first to use the term "I to Thou" when describing a particular type of relationship between two people, or between an individual and God. As we shall see, a healthy relationship is based on this type of a connection.

So what does it mean to say that a relationship has this unique quality? Buber described it in this way: "When I confront a human being as my You and speak the basic word I-You to him, then he is no thing among things, nor does he consist of things" (1970, 59).

Reread the previous sentence. Can you feel the depth of this type of a connection to another human being? This is the hallmark of an "I to Thou" relationship. This type of a connection is personal—very personal. It is not colored by what should be or what is supposed to be. When we meet and make contact on these terms, in this intimate way, we are relating to each other as the *subjects* of our conversation rather than as *objects*. We do not have an ulterior motive; our only purpose is to make contact. We are not trying to manipulate the person to validate us. We are not trying to regulate them to soothe our anxiety or trying to manipulate them for support. We don't need to, because we can support ourselves. We are simply present with them and with the experience we are having together. We are open to whatever happens, and we don't have an agenda or goal. Buber elaborates on this point: "The purpose of relationship is relationship itself—touching the You. For as soon as we touch a You, we are touched by a breath of eternal life" (1970, 112). This is the hidden reward of working Steps 8 through 10: we learn to make contact in a way that makes us feel we have been touched by the eternal breath of life.

My mentor, Dr. Kempler (1982), used to say, "To be more personal, we have to stop taking our partner's behavior personally." We have to get out of the way if we are going to be personal, if we are going to touch someone's Youness. In order to achieve this state of mind and to see the other person's true essence, we have to stop taking what they are saying or doing personally. When we are connected to another person in this way, it means that we are totally present with them in the here and now. Anything that subtracts from our total presence will downgrade the quality of our connection.

Making contact in this rich, alive, and meaningful way is at the heart of a healthy connection with another human being. This type of relationship isn't possible if we relate to people as objects that we can manipulate to satisfy our needs. This type of manipulative contact transforms our relationships into an "I to it" connection. In this case, we are looking at the other person as a source of approval or disapproval; we are not experiencing them as they are. The relationship is no longer personal. Their needs are irrelevant to us, unless, of course, making their needs relevant will help us get what we want. We objectify them. We don't care about them: we only care about what they can or cannot do for us. They lose any and all personal qualities because *we see them as we need them to be*. What we primarily care about is getting our needs satisfied. Narcissistic, isn't it? Well, the truth is, we all have narcissistic tendencies.

What drives us to have these types of human relations? If we dig deep down, we will discover that our emotional dependency is fueling this entire process. Because we do not know how to validate ourselves or soothe our anxiety, we try to regulate others so we don't have to feel anxious. Because we do not know how to support ourselves, we manipulate our environment to provide us with support. We manipulate the world to give us what we don't give to ourselves. This was the direction that our lives took when we rejected our real-self in favor of a false-self. Our false-self tried to soothe our anxiety by controlling and manipulating others to get what we thought we needed.

Our attitudes toward others, and our treatment of others, are shaped by our false-self. Dr. Karen Horney, a brilliant psychoanalyst, described the disturbances that take place in our human relations when we are living according to the specifications and rules of our false-self. She stated that we "see others in the light of the needs engendered by the pride system" (1950, 292). Remember, the pride system enacts and enforces the rules of the false-self.

The way we treat others is determined by the direction in which our anxiety propelled us to find a solution. Dr. Horney (1950, 292), after years of analyzing people, observed the following ways our attitudes toward others are influenced by our needs:

- Our need for admiration turns others into an admiring audience.
- Our need for magical help endows someone with mysterious magical abilities.

- Our need to be right makes someone else wrong, faulty, and fallible.
- Our need for triumph divides the world into followers or scheming adversaries.
- Our need to hurt someone with impunity turns others into being worthy of our abuse.
- Our need to minimize ourselves turns others into giants.

As you can see from this list, we do not see other people as they are; we see them as we need them to be to fulfill our purpose. We impose our script on them and cast them into the role we need. We don't *see* them, we *see them as we need them to be.*

This doesn't mean we are bad people; it means we are human beings who have taken the wrong turn early in life. The Steps are helping us find our way back. They are correcting the veer in our personal development.

Steps 8 and 9 do this by undoing our objectification of others and transforming them into a Thou in our lives. These Steps are teaching us to be more personal and present, to make full and alive contact with another person. They are teaching us to drop our expectations and meet people where they are at.

Steps 1–7 helped us develop a better relationship with ourselves. Without a better connection to ourselves, we can't have better human relations. If we do not experience ourselves as lovable, then it will be impossible to believe that anyone else could love us. So we had to get right with ourselves. We had to straighten out our "stinking thinking" and develop an understanding of the forces within us that influenced our behavior. We had to get honest with ourselves and learn how to use the best in us to look at the worst in us.

Working the Steps helps us reconstruct our self-understanding based on reality, instead of the distortions of reality that were caused by our anxiety. We now have a more positive self-concept because of our efforts to find a solution to our addiction. Steps 1–7 changed our relationship to ourselves and prepared us, mentally and spiritually, for Steps 8 through 10.

Dr. Jerry Greenwald, a very gifted psychotherapist, noted: "It is not possible for me to relate to others intimately and allow (enjoy) their full expression of themselves, if I have not yet discovered how to do this for myself. Intimacy of Two begins with intimacy of one" (1975, 63).

Our efforts in Step 8 begin with an honest and accurate self-evaluation. We make a list of all the people we have harmed and how we have harmed them. We reflect upon the wreckage of our past and motivate ourselves to right these wrongs, restore social justice, and make our victims whole. For many of us, this is a Herculean task. But because of our newfound connection with a power greater than ourselves, and because of our newfound ability to support ourselves, we set out to face those we've hurt.

This process helps us base our human relations on an "I to Thou" foundation. We give up playing games and make our human relations personal. We get in touch with our culpability and our responsibility.

Our compassion moves us to right these wrongs and to restore wholeness. We only delay or stop our amends if making them would do more harm than good. We learn to treat other people equally and make needs as important as our own. And we do this because it is the right thing to do.

Step 10 helps us maintain this new way of being and relating. Through a regular practice of honest self-evaluation, we monitor our behavior, and when we are wrong, we promptly clean up our side of the street. We aim at being the best we can be. We pressure ourselves to change, and in doing so, we find that others stop pressuring us to change. They don't need to change us anymore. We are now stepping up and being accountable to ourselves; we no longer need a mommy or daddy to keep us in line. We have taken total responsibility for our lives and the changes we need to make.

We've come a long way. We are trustworthy and capable of a healthy relationship based on a personal connection. Dr. Greenwald summarizes the hidden reward that we enjoy from being able to have an "I to Thou" relationship:

> Good contact with our Intimate Self and our Intimate Other provides enormous energy with which to relate to our world in a most satisfying, most meaningful, and creative fashion. It provides us with the ability to experience great joy and excitement because of the limitless potential for self-discovery and growth and the increasing ability to function in the world. This is the optimal condition for fulfillment of our self and for living a meaningful, nourishing life. (1975, 202)

A client of mine named Bernadette came to see me for a recovery check-up. She had been working a solid program in NA for over eight years but felt like she had reached a plateau. She had read my book on emotional sobriety and wanted to better understand her behavior in relations with other people. I asked her to describe a situation that bothered her. She stated that her seventeen-year-old daughter, Maya, was getting ready to go off to college. Maya was in the process of completing her applications, but had not yet written the essays that required her to describe herself and her reasons for selecting that particular school.

At the time we discussed this situation, Maya still had about three weeks remaining before the essay needed to be completed, but

Bernadette was getting anxious that she wasn't going to complete it in time. She told me that earlier that day she had been pressuring her daughter to work on the essay. Maya replied by telling her mom that she first needed to complete the homework that was due for her summer classes and then she would work on the essay. This wasn't good enough for Bernadette, and she demanded that Maya drop everything and get busy on the essay. Her daughter refused, and Bernadette grounded her.

I could see that Bernadette wasn't happy with her interaction with her daughter. I asked her what she didn't like about her behavior. She said that it just didn't feel right, and she didn't like being so controlling and punitive. I told her that I was glad she didn't like being this way, because the part of her that interacted with her daughter in that way was the worst in her, not the best. She agreed.

We focused on unpacking what happened. I used The Emotional Sobriety Inventory Form from the appendix in *12 Smart Things to Do When the Booze and Drugs Are Gone* to facilitate this process (Berger 2010). In the first column, Bernadette described the upsetting event exactly as you read it above. In the second column, she needed to identify the unhealthy dependency that was an undercurrent in her relationship with her daughter. What she identified, with my help, is that she wanted to regulate her anxiety by controlling Maya. Anxious that her daughter wasn't going to get in to the college of her choice, Bernadette nagged Maya in order to relieve her *own* personal anxiety, not to help her daughter.

In the third column, Bernadette had to identify the unreasonable expectation or demand that she placed on her daughter. This is always a difficult step: it's hard for us to admit that we are unreasonable. Bernadette struggled with this too. Finally, she realized her unreasonable expectation: that her daughter should do whatever Bernadette wanted her to do so that Bernadette wouldn't feel anxious. *She was manipulating her daughter for her own needs.* She didn't know how to soothe her own anxiety, so she wanted Maya to do it for her. She was turning to her daughter for nurturing. That isn't her daughter's job.

Bernadette realized she was wrong to do this, and when she saw Maya that night she immediately admitted she was wrong. She told her daughter that it was wrong to pressure her to take care of her mother's anxiety, and that it was Bernadette's job to learn how to soothe herself—not her daughter's job to make Bernadette feel better.

When we discussed how Bernadette was going to make amends, I suggested that she give her daughter permission to let her know whenever Bernadette was pressuring her. ("Mom, it is not my job to soothe your anxiety. That's your job, not mine!") She agreed and added that onto her amends.

After I had inquired about how things had gone, Bernadette sent me a touching e-mail. In it she described an incident after making amends where she had tried discouraging her daughter from getting an after-school job so she could focus on college applications. Her daughter reminded her mother that it was not her responsibility to alleviate her mother's anxiety.

Bernadette stopped manipulating Maya to soothe her own anxiety. That is Bernadette's job, not her daughter's. Being able to create "I to Thou" connections with those we love is a tremendous benefit and a valuable hidden reward from working Steps 8 through 10.

Let's now turn to the twelfth and final hidden reward of making amends and practicing self-evaluation.

Hidden Reward 12:
Being the Self That We Truly Are

You are probably amazed at the hidden rewards that you have discovered and experienced in your life as you've worked the Steps, especially Steps 8, 9, and 10. Let's take a moment and review the rewards we've discussed so far:

- We are staying in closer contact with our experience, which helps us function more fully. We are able to flow with our experience and satisfy our needs. We learn from our experience.
- We are honest and authentic. We don't play games, and we quit trying to be a self that we are not.
- We have taken responsibility to right our wrongs. We have compassion for those we hurt and do whatever is necessary to restore social justice. We know the true meaning of self-forgiveness and have sought forgiveness from others when appropriate.

- We are functioning with a sense of autonomy and emotional freedom. We stop holding people hostage and free ourselves from the emotional clutch of others. We don't do things to get validation from others, and instead do the right thing because it is the right thing to do.
- We value the process of being as an alternative to the mad obsession of always wanting more.
- We focus on being trustworthy, and because of this we enjoy healthier and more satisfying human relations.
- We understand the importance of being of value to others and of making a positive difference in our lives and in the lives of others.
- We strive to soothe our anxiety and regulate our emotions without manipulating others to do it for us. We have developed tools that help us recover our emotional balance when we lose it.
- Our self-esteem is better and our reputation with ourselves has improved.
- We have recovered our integrity and strive to integrate what we are learning intellectually and emotionally.
- We relate to others from an "I to Thou" perspective. We try not to take things personally in our relationships, and therefore our human relations are more intimate.

The path to discover these hidden rewards has been quite difficult and treacherous at times. But it has been well worth our trouble. If we have stayed the course, our lives are richer and we are more alive than ever. We have learned to support ourselves and let the best in us operate the rest of us. We have stopped the civil war between what we thought were incompatible parts of ourselves.

We practice daily self-evaluation and self-monitoring, and when we find ourselves out of line, we pull ourselves up and clean up our side of the street. Peace of mind and serenity are no longer strangers, but regular guests in our hearts and minds. We are at harmony with ourselves and others.

By weakening the destructive forces of addiction and the false-self, we have seen the constructive forces of our real-self grow. We have recovered the ability to actualize our human potential. The basic need we have for self-actualization is now flowing in our lives. It is encouraging and seeking our growth and maturation. It is driving us to reach our full human potential. It is motivating us to aim at doing our best and being our best.

Our real-self contains a spring of emotional forces, of constructive and positive energies, of self-directive and judiciary powers (Horney 1950). It contains an organic and spiritual wisdom that helps us discover the true purpose and meaning of our lives.

Our true-self is capable of making creative adjustments to the problems we encounter in life. This adjustment occurs when we have a healthy, uninterrupted flow with our experience—that is, when an emerging need is satisfied. It happens when we bring our full awareness to a problem we are having, without the interference of "shoulds" or "ought tos." We are then free to gather the necessary information we need about ourselves and our environment so we can invent creative ways to make contact and satisfy our needs.

Sometimes this means asserting ourselves, and sometimes it means admitting we are wrong. Our false-pride no longer interferes with our choices. Our actions are guided by the best in us instead of the worst in us. Because we can invent creative solutions to satisfy our needs, we don't need to manipulate anyone to take care of us or absorb our nonsense. This is what it means to *support ourselves*. It comes from living with the philosophy that it is the responsibility of each of us, and each of us alone, to respond to and satisfy our own needs. Instead of trying to get other people to listen to us, we listen to ourselves and take what we have to say seriously.

We also realize that it is our responsibility to set healthy boundaries. M. Scott Peck pointed out that responsibility has two sides to it: "To be free people we must assume total responsibility for ourselves, but in doing so must possess the capacity to reject responsibility that is not truly ours" (1978, 64). We are not responsible for the choices that other people make, nor for what other people do. We are responsible only for what *we* do or don't do.

Working the Steps has helped us recover our true-self. We have a new understanding of ourselves and our potential. We are no longer shackled by the performance demands placed on us by our false-self; we have liberated ourselves from its tyranny. We have become spontaneous and creative, and have reached a degree of ego-integrity. We thirst for knowledge of ourselves and the good life. We thirst for spiritual wisdom and seek experiences that will facilitate our growth.

We recognize that emotions such as pain, disappointment, conflict, grief, anger, shame, and guilt are parts of the human experience to be accepted, understood, and valued rather than suppressed or hidden. We no longer reject or disown a part of ourselves because it is perceived as incompatible with the rest of us. We search to bring this stranger into harmony with the rest of us because we know it is a part of us and that being whole is more important than living up to some idealized version of who we should be. We strive to honor ourselves, to accept ourselves, and to realize our true human potential.

We stand in wonder of who we are and what God has created. We are being the self that we truly are. We are centered and balanced. Fritz Perls recognized the importance of being centered in the self we truly are: "Without a center, everything goes on in the periphery and there is no place from which to work—from which to cope with the world. Without a center you are not alert. . . . Being grounded in oneself, is about the highest state a human being can achieve" (1969, 37).

Our new relationship with ourselves is an example of the whole being greater than the sum of its parts. This is the goal of our work: to come to know ourselves as we truly are—our true-self—and discard what we are not.

Our true-self isn't one self. We aren't fixed. We are a harmony of a population of selves, rather than being the clarity and simplicity of one rigid self. We are being and becoming simultaneously. Virginia Satir, a brilliant family therapist, made these remarks when describing how a healthy self functions:

> However I look and sound, whatever I say and do, and whatever I think and feel at a given moment in time is me. This is authentic and represents where I am at that moment in time. When I review later how I looked and sounded, what I said and did, and how I thought and felt, some parts may turn out to be unfitting. I can discard that which is unfitting, and keep what proved fitting and invent something new for that which I discarded. . . . I own me and therefore I can engineer me. (1975)

We have a growing pride in being our real-self: in being sensitive, open, teachable, curious, loving, assertive, passionate, realistic, autonomous, authentic, self-supportive, honest, trustworthy, alive, responsible, and creative. When we have problems with others, we are committed to finding mutually satisfying solutions. We enjoy balancing togetherness with individuality, letting the best in us operate the rest of us, and honoring our spirituality.

Evan had sat with me for many hours struggling with his most recent situation. His wife had been injured in a terrible car accident that left her a paraplegic. While he had some help in caring for her, most of the burden fell on his shoulders, and he was buckling under the strain. He had become irritable and impatient with her, and often fantasized about leaving her. He hated his life and the hand that they had been dealt. "When will it end?" he wondered.

The first thing we focused on in our sessions was to help him become aware of the rules he had about what was OK and what wasn't OK for him to feel. He felt guilty for being fed up with his wife, for being irritated, for wanting her to die. This isn't who he was supposed to be. He expected himself to be superhuman—always loving and understanding. He wasn't a saint after all, and this was causing him a tremendous amount of pain. He certainly didn't feel the way he thought he was supposed to feel.

We worked for months on this problem, and eventually Evan became aware of the impossible expectations and unrealistic performance demands he had imposed on himself. I helped him own the outrageous demands he placed on himself. He started to challenge these rules and develop an ability to accept himself as he was. He could see that he needed to let go of the rules that his false-self had imposed on him. These rules were killing him and preventing him from being his authentic-self.

As Evan let go of the self he wasn't and became his true-self, he was able to give expression to these painful emotions without judging himself for what he was feeling. Instead of rejecting these parts of him, he started to make peace with them. He found a way to be in harmony with these feelings. He was recovering his integrity: he was recovering his true-self.

What Evan couldn't see before is that he was an incredible and loving man who was making a tremendous sacrifice to honor his commitment and relationship to the woman he loved. His feelings didn't define him or take away from who he really was: they were just a normal reaction to being a caregiver in this kind of a situation.

As he started to accept and support himself, he became more creative in how he and his wife spent time together. He stopped letting her injury determine what he could and couldn't do with her. He learned how to do guided imagery, and they started taking these journeys together. He'd put on some of their favorite music and describe to her how they were dancing together in one of their favorite locations. These sessions would often bring a tear or smile to both of them. He creatively adjusted to their situation by letting go of who he thought he should be. He let who he truly was take over the show.

Evan left me an e-mail after we terminated therapy. He wanted to thank me. He was happier than he had ever been in his recovery. He wasn't letting his wife's injury define their existence any longer, and he wasn't letting his false-self dictate who he was supposed to be. He was free to be the self he truly was. He worked hard at his emotional sobriety and at establishing his emotional freedom and autonomy. He centered himself, and this made all the difference in the world. He told me that he finally had found peace of mind and serenity regardless of his unfortunate situation.

Now that we've gotten to know the twelve hidden rewards we experience by owning up to our past behavior and becoming the self that we are meant to be, let's learn how this process propels us forward to do even more in our lives and in our recovery.

Understanding the Promises

Many psychologists and other health care professionals now recognize the incredible transformation that occurs when we work the Twelve Steps. Working the Steps initiates a powerful chain reaction caused by mixing psychological and spiritual forces in a unique way. This chain reaction alters how we function in relation to ourselves and others. Through a profound spiritual awakening, we are completely reconstructed. Here's what happens to us when we work Steps 1–9.

We shatter our reliance on a false-self and accept the reality that we can neither control nor manage our addiction. Instead of dedicating the rest of our lives to actualizing an idealized image of who we should be or trying to control something we are powerless over, we begin a journey of actualizing *ourselves*. We find a power greater than ourselves to turn to for guidance and strength. We commit ourselves to constructing a more positive self-image and repairing our damaged self-esteem.

Instead of taking the path of least resistance, we embrace the pain and disgust that arises from facing the worst in ourselves. We motivate ourselves to clean up our side of the street, regardless of whether our attitude is reciprocated by those who have hurt us. We make a sincere effort to right our wrongs and take responsibility for the harm we have done to others. We discover the best in us by facing the worst in us.

We learn to center ourselves by doing the right thing because it is the right thing to do. We stop looking for approval, perfect security, and perfect love. We become more spiritual, emotionally balanced, and grounded in reality. We learn to stand on our own two feet and validate ourselves or pull ourselves up when we're wrong. We unhook our dependency on others for our self-esteem, and we take corrective action to repair our damaged self-esteem. We develop a practice of self-reflection to evaluate what we are doing well and put ourselves in check when we are doing the wrong things.

We come to know ourselves as human *beings*, populated with a lot of different characters or parts to ourselves. We establish harmony between the warring factions within ourselves. We practice keeping our side of the street clean in human relations and learn to be in sync with others. We come to accept our imperfections and ask for help when we need it. Our goal is to take the best possible attitude toward ourselves and others.

When I stand back and look at this incredible process, I am overwhelmed with wonder and gratitude. We have been given a remarkable gift: a formula for change. The secret of turning lead into gold, weakness into strength, and a destructive wound into a sacred wound has been revealed to us. We've found redemption in our self-destruction.

The effects of working these Steps are far-reaching. These effects are spelled out in the Big Book of Alcoholics Anonymous, and known to Twelve-Steppers as simply the "Promises." As you are about to see, the "Promises" are the direct result of the therapeutic forces that gave us the twelve hidden rewards we discovered in Steps 8, 9, and 10. Here they are:

> We are going to know a new freedom and a new happiness. We will not regret the past nor wish to shut the door on it. We will comprehend the word serenity and we will know peace. No matter how far down the scale we have gone, we will see how our experience can benefit others. That feeling of uselessness and self-pity will disappear. We will lose interest in selfish things and gain interest in our fellows. Self-seeking will slip away. Our whole attitude and outlook upon life will change. Fear of people and of economic insecurity will leave us. We will intuitively know how to handle situations which used to baffle us. We will suddenly realize that God is doing for us what we could not do for ourselves. (*Alcoholics Anonymous* 2001, 83–84)

Let's unpack these promises one by one, and see how the process of making amends and experiencing the rewards of doing so helps us live out these promises.

We are going to know a new freedom and a new happiness.
Our false-self and our addiction robbed us of true freedom. We were imprisoned by their forces. We lived to use and used to live. We compulsively lived up to an idealized self-image instead of actualizing our real-self. We were driven by false-pride to be the self that we weren't.

The Steps help us release the shackles of our false-self and break the hold that addiction had on our lives. By working the Steps, we recover our true-self, and with it the freedom to actualize our true potential. By letting go of perfection, we free ourselves from the tyranny of the false-self. We focus on building character and being open and honest, and we aim at developing the best possible attitude toward ourselves and others.

Our new happiness is found in being who we are rather than in actualizing a concept of who we should be. We are spontaneous and flow with our experience. We learn to take care of ourselves because we stay in close contact with our feelings. We no longer torture ourselves with pressure from unrealistic high expectations of performance, and instead measure ourselves by the progress we've made. We are free from the rules and dictates of our false-self and therefore are much happier with ourselves and more satisfied with life.

We develop an emotional freedom in our human relations. We learn to unhook our emotional dependency on people, places, and things. Instead of manipulating others to validate us or support us, we validate and support ourselves. We learn to center ourselves in doing what's right because it is the right thing to do.

We stop taking hostages in relationships and start building authentic relations based on an "I to Thou" attitude. We relate to others as equals rather than setting them on pedestals or putting them down so that we can feel superior to them. We hold on to ourselves while being in close contact with others. We learn to hold on to our autonomy while preserving a connection with others. We discover that mature love says, "I want you because I love you."

We will not regret the past nor wish to shut the door on it.

We have seen that by being honest with ourselves, we can learn from the past. Our honest reflection can help us understand who we are and who we aren't. Our understanding of our past can help us identify certain themes in our behavior that point to the work we need to do to grow up. We have found that we need to stop judging ourselves if we want to learn from our past behavior.

When we avoided facing who we had become, we shut the door on reality. We didn't want to see how we used others for our benefit, or face how our selfishness and self-centeredness turned us into cruel and sadistic monsters. *We regretted the past because it reflected the mess we had made of our lives.* No one likes to see how wrong they have been or face the mistakes they have made.

However, once we face the worst in us, we discover the best in us. We discover the compassionate part of ourselves that we had shut down because it would have created a cognitive dissonance. As we recover our true-self, we step up to restore justice, to make whole those we have harmed. We look at the patterns of our behavior so we can become aware of our shortcomings. We work on being trustworthy, taking responsibility for our behavior, and building a more positive self-concept.

As we clean up the wreckage of our past and aim at incorporating the best possible attitude toward ourselves and others, our past no longer reflects a poor self-image that we are ashamed to see. It now reflects our commitment to a better way of life. It reflects our commitment to recovery and to honoring our true-self. It reflects something positive about ourselves.

Having worked these Steps, we see ourselves striving to be honest, authentic, responsible, compassionate, helpful, loving, and forgiving. We see ourselves in a very different light: as perfectly imperfect. We humbly accept ourselves as we are. We can look straight into our own eyes without being ashamed of who we see, because we experience ourselves as evolving and maturing. We are committed to spiritual progress and have given up the quest for perfection and power.

We have developed a new appreciation and understanding of ourselves and our human potential. Our possible self has become our actual self.

We will comprehend the word serenity
and we will know peace.

Our false-self rejected any part of us that didn't fit with its idealized image of who we should be. We were in constant conflict with ourselves. We battled with any parts of ourselves that didn't fit the specifications our false-self dictated. It is impossible to have serenity or peace if a civil war is raging inside us.

Our internal battles were imposed on others. We expected others to conform to our unrealistic expectations too. We believed that if others really cared for us, they'd submit to our rules. This created conflicts in our human relations. We insisted others do it our way, and when they didn't submit to our demands, there was a price to pay.

Because of the work we do, we stop trying to live up to these ridiculous expectations or to impose our expectations on others. Acceptance, tolerance, progress, and reality replace intolerance, perfectionism, expectations, and ideals. We befriend ourselves and find peace between what seemed to be incompatible parts of ourselves. We strive for "I to Thou" relationships based on mutual respect. We respect differences and monitor when we are out of line. We don't let unfinished business pile up and stress us out. We do spot checks and daily inventories to ensure that we stay right with ourselves and with others.

Our serenity and peace is rooted in a new and healthier relation with ourselves and others.

No matter how far down the scale we have gone, we will
see how our experience can benefit others. That feeling of
uselessness and self-pity will disappear.

Our culture values ascending, not descending. We wanted to rise to the top. We wanted success, to succeed and be the best. We dreaded failing, hitting bottom, and defeat. But we needed to shed those old ideas or we would wallow in self-pity and self-loathing.

Working the Steps helps us turn our failures into valuable lessons. Our wrongs help us discover what is right. We integrate the lessons we learned from our mistakes to better cope with life and to better understand ourselves. We discover that the problem itself was never the problem. The problem came from how we dealt with it: the problem was our attitude. Learning from our failures is critical to our growth in recovery.

When we share our uncensored experience with a newcomer, we help them identify their problem and give them hope that there is a solution. We find that being ourselves, openly and authentically, is of great value. We don't need to be a self we are not in order to be of value. Real value comes from being the self that we truly are, and sharing it openly and authentically.

Given that all of our experience, both the positive and negative, is of value, the feeling of uselessness and self-pity disappears. We stop measuring our worth by what we don't have, or how little money we possess, or the car we don't have, or what we haven't achieved. Although possessions and achievements are nice, they don't define our value. We find that our true value lies in who we are, in being real, in how we work our program, in how we live our lives, and in how we struggle to keep our integrity. Our perspective was out of balance. We valued things more than we valued integrity.

We find that the best way we can help others who are struggling to find the right path to recovery is by sharing our uncensored and raw experience with them. Our weaknesses become a source of healing, our failures become a source of identification, and our mistakes become a source of humility and wisdom. We receive other people as they are. They don't have to be something they are not to be welcomed or accepted. Our humble experience welcomes them as they are. We make a difference because of who we are, not because of what we have. It quickly becomes clear that our experience does benefit others.

We will lose interest in selfish things and gain interest in our fellows. Self-seeking will slip away.

When our false-self was in control, we were self-centered. We were concerned with getting approval, love, or power, and we were focused on having more and more and more. We were only concerned about what someone could or couldn't do for us. We relied on people as sources of love or validation.

Once the Steps shatter our reliance on our false-self and it loosens its grip on us, we can see that there is more to life than we imagined. We begin to let go of our old ideas and replace them with updated spiritual versions. We begin to see that the more we give away what we have, the more we can keep it. This didn't make any sense to our false-self, but it makes real sense to our emerging spiritual self. We begin to see the power of paradox: the more we get out of our self, the more we find ourselves; the more we surrender control, the better we feel; the more we give, the more we receive.

Being of service to others becomes an important part of our lives. Our first thought isn't about what we are going to get out of a certain situation, but rather how we can be of value to others in the situation. We strive to "sweeten the pot" whenever we can.

We gain interest in our fellows beyond what they can or can't do for us. We relate to them from an "I to Thou" perspective based on mutual respect and authenticity. We strive to actualize our potential and the potential of others. We become true citizens of the world and valuable members of the recovery community. We have become a part of the solution.

Our whole attitude and outlook upon life will change.

Working the Steps creates a total transformation of our approach to life. We experience a 180-degree shift in our thinking and in our way of being. We become more concerned with being trustworthy, present, honest, authentic, open, and willing. Instead of using our traits to manipulate others, we use them to actualize our potential and the potential of others.

By working the Steps, we learn to convert the traits we once used to manipulate others into ways of connecting with others and actualizing our potential and theirs. If we manipulated others by being a "nice guy," we now use our warmth to actualize our contact with others. If we were the bully, intimidating others to submit to our will, we learn instead to be assertive, respecting our rights and the rights of others. If we manipulated others by being a dictator, we learn to become a leader. If we rescued others, we learn to be a guide.

As manipulators we were deceptive, rigid, controlling, cynical, and unaware. When we decided to actualize our potential, we became honest, transparent, spontaneous, optimistic, aware, free, trusting, and trustworthy. This is a major shift in our way of being. We stop taking from others and start developing a give-and-take attitude.

We aim at letting the best in us operate the rest of us. We focus on being constructive, not destructive. We are concerned about the feelings of others and what they want, rather than manipulating them to validate us. We let the best in us take the lead in our interactions with others and do the talking for us.

We listen to ourselves rather than demand that others listen to us. We pressure ourselves to change rather than pressure others to change to our liking. We regulate our own feelings and stop trying to regulate everyone else. We forgive rather than manipulate others into forgiving us. We comfort ourselves rather than manipulate others into comforting us by doing what we want.

We lick our own wounds and take responsibility for what we want, rather than ensure we are never going to be disappointed and blame everyone else for what happens. We center ourselves by doing the right thing because it is the right thing to do.

We move from needing to have a fixed position to having one of adaptability, from a rigid structure to flexibility, from wanting things to remain the same to embracing the philosophy that life is a process.

We experience an entire psychic shift in our attitude and behavior. We become flexible and creative in how we deal with our feelings, difficult situations, and human relations. We come to realize that our happiness does not lie in the experience we are having, but rather in our relationship to that experience. We let go of the immature idea that life should be easy and accept the reality that life is difficult. We learn to let go of our expectations about how life is supposed to be, and instead accept the notion that it is our job to cope with whatever life expects from us. We find that our answer to any question is found in right action and right conduct.

We come to realize that Dr. Frankl was right when he said, "The way in which a man accepts his fate and all the suffering it entails, the way in which he takes up his cross, gives him ample opportunity—even under the most difficult circumstances—to add a deeper meaning to his life" (1984, 76). We are adding deeper meaning to our lives through working the Steps.

We know that we can stay clean and sober under any and all conditions or circumstances whatsoever, as long as we remain grounded in our program and in our relationship with a power greater than ourselves.

Fear of people and of economic insecurity will leave us.

We were afraid of people because we projected onto them our own self-judgment. Projection is a psychological mechanism that takes our own unwanted or disowned attitudes or feelings and attributes them to the environment or someone in it.

For good reason, we didn't like ourselves. We were selfish and self-centered manipulators. We became a juggernaut of self-destruction and left in our wake broken hearts, betrayal, fear, disappointment, abuse, anxiety, distrust, suspicion, and frustration. We secretly hated ourselves for who we had become and were ashamed that we didn't do anything to change.

In early recovery, our self-hate is a major issue and colors all of our interactions, decisions, and human relations. We believe that other people are judging us as harshly as we are judging ourselves. We fear that we are going to be exposed as the phony we knew we were. Once we admit we are phonies, we are no longer afraid of being exposed. Once we face our self-hate and shame, we no longer believe other people are looking down on us. Once we own our true feelings about ourselves, we stop imagining that other people are judging us.

As we work the Steps, we become honest and face the worst in us. We take responsibility for the damage we have done and make a sincere effort to correct our wrongs. We develop a more positive self-concept based on right action and right conduct. Our fear of others ceases because we are no longer at odds with ourselves. We accept ourselves as we are, and also know that we are evolving and actualizing our true human potential. We no longer disown parts of ourselves, and therefore we don't have a need to project.

While economic security is important, we realize that we had the cart before the horse. We made "having things" the basis for our economic security instead of realizing that true security comes from who we are, not what we have. *We* are our most important source of security: it isn't out there in the world for us to procure. When our house is in order, life flows and provides us with everything we need.

Instead of trying to wrestle economic or emotional security from life, we focus on keeping our side of the street clean and try to be of value whenever we can. Instead of making life about what we need, we make life about actualizing our potential and the potential of others. Our security is no longer determined by economics, but by right action and right conduct. We learn that focusing on the process is more important than focusing on the outcome.

We will intuitively know how to handle situations which used to baffle us.

Because the Steps dethrone the false-self, our real-self emerges. The energies that were hijacked and aimed at actualizing our false-self are recovered, and are now driving us toward self-realization (Horney 1950). We recover our true-self, and with it our God-given intuition.

Our false-self made it impossible to be in touch with our intuition; our intuition was not accessible as a source of information because our false-self, which was concerned with power and being in control, interfered with it. We overmanaged ourselves and controlled others. We couldn't get out of our way long enough to let our intuition guide us, or to listen to what our intuition was telling us to do.

Our false-self had an agenda and wouldn't let anything interfere with getting from our environment what it thought we needed. Our false-self made it seem to us that there was never enough of what we thought we needed. There wasn't, because we were out of touch with what we really needed. We lost sight of ourselves and our real needs and replaced them with the aims of our false-self.

Remember the discussion of the cycle of experience in chapter 1? Our intuition is grounded in the cycle of experience. We possess an inner, God-given wisdom that will guide us to satisfy our needs, as long as we listen to it. When we stay in close contact with our experience, our intuition will tell us what we need to do in any given situation to take care of ourselves. Our body will speak its mind, our soul will speak its mind, and our heart will speak its mind. If we listen to ourselves, we will know our truth. We will be able to respond to any situation, creatively and spontaneously, because we will be staying in close contact with our experience.

Dr. Fritz Perls believed that staying in touch with ourselves and being aware of what we are experiencing in a situation is crucial to coping better with life: "If you understand the situation you are in, and let the situation which you are in control your actions, then you learn how to cope with life" (1969, 19). Our intuition will inform and guide our actions, but we have to let go and trust the cycle of experience. We will intuitively know how to handle situations that used to baffle us because we are listening to our inner wisdom. We learn to flow with our experience.

We surrender the need to control outcomes and start trusting our inner wisdom to tell us how to handle any given situation. We find that we can creatively respond to our needs and to the demands of any situation, because we trust our real-self to take right action.

We will suddenly realize that God is doing for us what we could not do for ourselves.

God has been very busy in our lives. Our Step work opens the door to an inner wisdom. Our inward searching helps us come to know ourselves more intimately than ever before. We make many important self-discoveries on this journey.

We come to see how we fabricated a self that we thought would be the answer to our problems. We seek to understand our addicted-self and how it conspired with our false-self to create a juggernaut of self-destruction. We make a searching and fearless moral inventory of the self that we had become, our false-self, and become acquainted with our possible self—our true-self, or real-self. Right action and right conduct help us recover our true-self. This process has put us in touch with the mystery, with God.

Dr. James Bugental (1978), a very talented existential-humanistic psychotherapist, made the following observation:

> God is a word that points to our ineffable subjectivity, to the unimaginable potential that lies within each of us, to the aspirations which well up within us for greater truth and vividness of living, to our compassion for the tragedy of the human condition, to our pride in the undestroyed but endlessly assaulted dignity and to something more. To the sense of mystery which we always live if we are truly aware and to the dedication to explore that mystery which is the very essence of being human. (139)

Developing our awareness helped us become conscious of many things that we did not want to see. But it has also helped us become conscious of something that is much bigger than us, an internal wisdom that seems to be organic and connected to God. M. Scott Peck (1978) stated that we can find a wisdom greater than ourselves inside of ourselves.

In my own personal journey, I can see that God has been doing for me what I couldn't do for myself. If you want further evidence of this, go to a Twelve Step meeting and look around the room. You will see men and women who at one time were dying from their addiction and who are now living incredible lives.

I have no doubt that my life has been guided by a wisdom far greater than what I consciously possess. My experience writing this book is a wonderful example of how this process operates in my life. When I sit down to write I discover what needs to be said. My writing comes from a part of me that I am not conscious of. There is another part of me that is shaping the ideas and concepts I am trying to communicate to you. It's like I become a channel of a wisdom that is far greater than my own. I am not in charge; there is a force inside running the show. A force that is beyond my conscious mind, that is wiser than me.

M. Scott Peck (1978) expressed the notion that we can connect in God through the interface of our consciousness and our unconsciousness. God speaks to us through our unconscious mind. This means that God has always been within us. We cut ourselves off from God's wisdom when we took control of our lives and fabricated a self to get what we thought we needed. We let our anxiety drive us to develop a self that we were not because we didn't trust in our inner wisdom. We betrayed ourselves and alienated ourselves from our real-self, from the inner wisdom that we possess. We alienated ourselves from God. When we recover our lost true-self, we recover our inner wisdom. We recover our accessibility to God's grace and wisdom. We become aware that God is doing for us what our false-self could never accomplish.

We are guided to clean house and make amends to those we hurt. Right action and right conduct helps us find real peace of mind and serenity.

What's Next?

This book has focused on the first ten Steps of the Twelve Step program, and this second part of the book helped you understand that special impact of the amends made through Steps 8, 9, and 10. We have seen how honesty, open-mindedness, and willingness set in motion a very powerful force of change inherent in the Twelve Steps. We have discussed the twelve hidden rewards embedded in making amends and in developing a practice of self-awareness and self-monitoring. We have seen how these forces have transformed our lives and delivered to us a set of unimaginable "Promises." Our work is far from over. There are two final Steps we need to take.

Step 11 continues the expansion of our consciousness, and through prayer and meditation, deepens our understanding of our true-self and how God operates in our lives. It reads: "Sought through prayer and meditation to improve our conscious contact with God *as we understand Him,* praying only for knowledge of His will for us and the power to carry that out" (*Alcoholics Anonymous* 2001, 59).

Recovery is a process, not an event. We must continue to grow and understand ourselves. We must continue to actualize our potential and to access the healing forces that are operating within us. We must continue to honor our real-self as that central inner force which is the source of our growth and evolution.

Step 12 is about integrating the practices we have developed in the first eleven Steps into everything we do, and helping those who still suffer. Step 12 reads: "Having had a spiritual awakening as the result of these steps, we tried to carry this message to alcoholics, and to practice these principles in all our affairs" (*Alcoholics Anonymous* 2001, 60).

I have previously spoken of the value of serving a cause greater than ourselves. Serving others becomes a powerful source of self-esteem. Step 12 provides us with a purpose for our lives and a way of creating meaning in our lives. We are encouraged to carry this message to those who are still suffering. Having a purpose in our lives and a way to create meaning in our lives becomes two more pillars for our self-esteem, which adds to a more solid sense of self.

Integration is also essential to our recovery. We must integrate what we know with what we do. We have to understand these principles on both an intellectual and an emotional level. When we integrate this information, it becomes a part of who we are. We no longer work the program; the program works us. Our behavior as a member of our recovery fellowship is seamless and indistinguishable from how we function at home, at work, or in our community. When we integrate these principles into all our affairs, they become a part of our actual self.

Summary

We have discovered a better use for all that energy we put into our addiction, into manipulating ourselves and others, and into actualizing an idealized image. We can use this rediscovered energy to recover our true-self, and to realize and actualize ourselves and our true human potential.

Working Steps 8, 9, and 10 is not easy, nor are these Steps meant for the faint of heart. They require courage and faith. But they will work, if you work them. They will help you break out of your psychic prison and find true freedom in your life. They will help you become the possible self that you have glimpsed in your recovery.

I implore you to never give up on finding your real-self. Recovery is a difficult path to trek, but it is well worth your efforts. Don't give up if you lose your way, or if you relapse. Don't expect yourself to work the Steps perfectly. I am reminded that "no one among us has been able to maintain anything like perfect adherence to these principles. We are not saints. The point is, that we are willing to grow along spiritual lines. . . . We claim spiritual progress rather than spiritual perfection" (*Alcoholics Anonymous* 2001, 60).

If you want real peace of mind and serenity, then clean house, make amends, and keep your side of the street clean. Help others, and get help when you get stuck. And let the best in you run the rest of you. The rewards are great: share them freely with others, and they will grow in value.

The first ten Steps have helped us recover our lost true-self and helped us develop healthier relationships. We aim at having the best possible attitude toward ourselves and others. The personal transformation taking place within us is truly remarkable.

Epilogue

I need to make amends to you. There is one person I forgot to mention who deserves equal consideration on our list: *us.* We need to make amends to ourselves too.

Despite my years in recovery and considerable experience helping others, making self-amends is still somewhat of a blind spot for me. In fact, this parallels my experience working Step 8. After presenting the list of the people I had harmed to my sponsor, Tom, he looked it over and said, "Someone is missing on your list."

"You've got to be kidding," I thought to myself. You see, I responded defensively because I had spent several hours working on the list and thought I did a "perfect job." I imagined that I was going to be given an "A" grade from Tom, but instead he said I missed identifying someone important. (Being perfect had always been a driving force in my life, and it reared its ugly head many times while working the Steps.)

"Who did I leave out?" I wondered.

Tom sensed that I was feeling defensive, and he told me to calm down and let him finish his thought. "You forgot to include yourself.

You hurt yourself as much as you hurt anyone else—maybe even more!"

At that point, I started to cry. When I was making my list, I never considered the harm I had inflicted upon myself. It was as though I didn't count. I was invisible, expendable. It never crossed my mind to look at the nature of my relationship with myself.

The moment Tom shared this thought with me, I knew he was right. I had hurt myself too. I needed to make amends to Allen as much as I needed to make amends to the other people on my list.

We have abused ourselves for many years. We abandoned our real-self in favor of an engineered self based on an idealized image. We compromised our integrity, our personal values, and our trustworthiness. We embarrassed ourselves and disappointed those who cared about us by using their love to manipulate them. We sold ourselves short and stunted our growth by taking the path of least resistance. We had sex with people we didn't want to because we needed their approval or because they had drugs. We poisoned our bodies and our souls. We let fear, anxiety, greed, and power control our lives. We have let the worst in us run the rest of us.

We have not protected or honored ourselves. We treated ourselves worse than anyone we harmed. So we need to be included on the list of people we need to make whole.

The question becomes, "How do we make amends to ourselves?" I have several suggestions.

Making Amends to Ourselves

First of all, by working Steps 8, 9, and 10, we are making amends to ourselves. The process of making amends restores our integrity. It makes us whole again because we are honoring ourselves. We are letting the best in us take the lead in our lives.

By managing our ongoing vulnerability to addiction on a daily basis, we are making amends to ourselves and protecting ourselves. When we attend a meeting or reach out to our sponsor, we are making amends to ourselves. When we make a mistake and take responsibility for it, we are making amends to ourselves. When we reach out and help someone who is still suffering, or when we stop the worst in us from destroying a relationship, we are making amends to ourselves. Any action that we take to support or realize our true-self is making amends to ourselves.

There is another thing we can do to make amends to ourselves, as you will see when I describe what happened recently when I met with Melinda.

Melinda has been clean and sober for about nine months. She currently resides in a very good women's sober living program in Southern California. She has three children who are being cared for by her parents. Melinda is thirty-six years old and started drinking and using twenty-two years ago. She has been through hell and back with her addiction, and has left a wake of destruction in her path. She has recently been working on Step 8.

She started our latest session by stating that she was eager to begin the process of making amends to those people she has hurt. Melinda most desperately wanted to make amends to her parents, but she wanted to do it in one of our sessions instead of during the Sunday afternoon family visits at her sober living residence. We had been planning on having a family therapy session with her mom and dad in the near future, but she said they would be out of town for the next several weeks, so the family session would have to wait.

As I sat with her contemplating what to do next, I realized that she had overlooked making amends to herself just like I did. I mentioned that she could start making amends to someone who was already present in the session. She looked at me and said, "I haven't done anything to hurt you, have I?" I quickly clarified what I meant. "No, you haven't done anything to me, but you have hurt yourself."

She got it, just like I got it. "Dah," she said. "How do I make amends to myself?" she asked.

"Well," I said, "you could put Melinda over in that empty chair and make amends to her for not taking better care of her and for not protecting her."

She did just that. She started talking to herself and telling her how sorry she was for having failed herself. She listed situation after situation where she failed to protect herself and ended up hurting herself. She began to heal the wounds inflicted by her self-destructiveness and her addiction.

You can do this type of an exercise as well. You can use an empty chair if you'd like, or write a letter to yourself. This can begin the process of healing and making yourself whole. But supporting and honoring your true-self with right action and right conduct are the ultimate ways to make amends to yourself.

I hope that you will take full advantage of the opportunity that the Twelve Steps give you to reconstruct healthier human relations and repair your damaged self-esteem. Remember, you have made many mistakes, but you are not a mistake. Your real-self deserves a chance to be realized.

Let the best in you heal the rest of you.

Appendix

Steps 8 and 9: Inventory Form

Name the person you have harmed and identify the type of relationship you had with him or her.	Describe in detail what you did and what happened.	Identify the type of harm you caused that person: was it physical, emotional, spiritual, or financial? (There will often be more than one type of harm.)	Write out your amends, what you need to take responsibility for in terms of the harm you have done to that person, and how you can restore his or her wholeness.

References and Recommended Reading

Alcoholics Anonymous, 4th ed. 2001. New York: Alcoholics Anonymous World Services.

Amodeo, J. 1994. *Love and Betrayal.* New York: Ballantine Books.

Arnold, R. A. 1977. "AA's 12 Steps as a Guide to 'Ego Integrity.'" *Journal of Contemporary Psychotherapy* 9 (1): 62–77.

Beisser, A. 1970. "The Paradoxical Theory of Change." In *Gestalt Therapy Now* (Eds. J. Fagan & I. L. Shepherd). New York: Harper & Row.

Berger, A. 2006. *Love Secrets Revealed: What Happy Couples Know about Having Great Sex, Deep Intimacy and Lasting Connections.* Deerfield Beach, FL: HCI Books.

Berger, A. 2008. *12 Stupid Things That Mess Up Recovery.* Center City, MN: Hazelden.

Berger, A. 2010. *12 Smart Things to Do When the Booze and Drugs Are Gone.* Center City, MN: Hazelden.

Branden, N. 1981. *The Psychology of Romantic Love.* New York: Bantam Books.

Branden, N. 1985. *Honoring the Self: Self-Esteem and Personal Transformation.* New York: Bantam Books.

Branden, N. 1994. *The Six Pillars of Self-Esteem*. New York: Bantam Books.

Branden, N. 1996. *Taking Responsibility: Self-Reliance and the Accountable Life*. New York: Fireside Books.

Buber, M. 1970. *I and Thou*. Translated by Walter Kaufman. New York: Charles Scribner's Sons.

Bugental, J. F. T. 1978. *Psychotherapy and Process: The Fundamentals of an Existential-Humanistic Approach*. New York: Random House.

Bugental, J. F. T. 1987. *The Art of the Psychotherapist*. New York: W.W. Norton.

Flores, P. J. 1977. *Group Psychotherapy with Addicted Populations: An Integration of Twelve-Step and Psychodynamic Theory*, 2nd ed. Binghamton, NY: Haworth Press.

Frank, J. D. 1963. *Persuasion and Healing: A Comparative Study of Psychotherapy*. New York: Schocken Books.

Frankl, V. E. 1984. *Man's Search for Meaning: An Introduction to Logotherapy*. 3rd ed. New York: Simon and Schuster.

Fromm, E. 1956. *The Art of Loving*. New York: Harper & Row.

Fromm, E. 1976. *To Have or To Be?* New York: Harper & Row.

Goble, F. 1971. *The Third Force: The Psychology of Abraham Maslow*. New York: Pocket Books.

Gorski, T. 1989. *Understanding the Twelve Steps: A Guide for Counselors, Therapists, and Recovering People*. Independence, MO: Herald House.

Greenwald, J. 1975. *Creative Intimacy: How to Break the Patterns That Poison Your Relationships*. New York: Simon and Schuster.

Helgoe, R. S. 2002. *Hierarchy of Recovery: From Abstinence to Self-Actualization*. Center City, MN: Hazelden.

Horney, K. 1950. *Neurosis and Human Growth: The Struggle toward Self-Realization*. New York: W.W. Norton.

Houston, G. 1990. *The Red Book of Gestalt Therapy*. London: Rochester Foundation.

Kaighan, H. 2010. *Twelve Steps to Spiritual Awakening: Enlightenment for Everyone*. Torrance, CA: Capizon Publishing.

Kempler, W. 1982. Personal communication.

Kerr, M. E., and M. Bowen. 1988. *Family Evaluation: An Approach Based on Bowen Theory*. New York: W.W. Norton.

Larsen, E. 1985. *Stage II Recovery: Life Beyond Addiction*. New York: Harper Collins Publishers.

Latner, J. 1973. *The Gestalt Therapy Book: A Holistic Guide to the Theory, Principles and Techniques of Gestalt Therapy Developed by Frederick S. Perls and Others*. New York: Bantam Books.

Luskin, F. 2002. *Forgive for Good: A Proven Prescription of Health and Happiness*. San Francisco: Harper San Francisco.

Maslow, A. H. 1954. *Motivation and Personality*. New York: Harper & Row.

Maslow, A. H. 1962. *Toward a Psychology of Being*. New York: Van Nostrand.

Peck, M. S. 1978. *The Road Less Traveled*. New York: Touchstone.

Peck, M. S. 1987. *The Different Drum: Community Making and Peace*. New York: Touchstone.

Perls, F. 1969. *Gestalt Therapy Verbatim*. Moab, UT: Real People Press.

Perls, F. 1976. *The Gestalt Approach & Eye Witness to Therapy*. New York: Bantam Books.

Perls, F., R. F. Hefferline, and P. Goodman. 1977. *Gestalt Therapy*. New York: Bantam Books.

Polster, E. 2005. *A Population of Selves: A Therapeutic Exploration of Personal Diversity*. Gouldsboro, ME: Gestalt Journal Press.

Polster, E., and M. Polster. 1973. *Gestalt Therapy Integrated: Contours of Theory and Practice*. New York: Brunner/Mazel.

Rogers, C. R. 1961. *On Becoming a Person: A Therapist's View of Psychotherapy.* New York: Houghton Mifflin.

Rohr, R. 2011. *Breathing Under Water: Spirituality and the Twelve Steps.* Cincinnati, OH: St. Anthony Messenger Press.

Satir, V. 1972. *Peoplemaking.* Palo Alto, CA: Science and Behavioral Books.

Satir, V. 1975. *Self Esteem.* Berkeley, CA: Celestial Arts.

Satir, V. 1978. *Your Many Faces: The First Step to Being Loved.* Berkeley, CA: Celestial Arts.

Schenker, M. D. 2009. *A Clinician's Guide to 12 Step Recovery: Integrating 12-Step Programs into Psychotherapy.* New York: W.W. Norton.

Schnarch, D. 1997. *Passionate Marriage: Keeping Love and Intimacy Alive in Committed Relationships.* New York: W.W. Norton.

Schnarch, D. 2009. *Intimacy and Desire: Awaken the Passion in Your Relationship.* New York: Beaufort Books.

Shostrom, E. 1968. *Man, the Manipulator: The Inner Journey from Manipulation to Actualization.* New York: Bantam Books.

Tamerin, J. S., and C. P. Neumann. 1974. "Psychological Aspects of Treating Alcoholism." *Alcohol Health and Research World* (Spring): 14–18.

Tiebout, H. 1999. *Harry Tiebout: The Collected Writings.* Center City, MN: Hazelden.

Tronick, E. Z., and J. F. Cohn. 1989. "Infant-Mother Face-to-Face Interaction: Age and Gender Difference in Coordination and the Occurrence of Miscoordination." *Child Development* 60 (1): 85–92.

Twelve Steps and Twelve Traditions. 1981. New York: Alcoholics Anonymous World Services, Inc.

Wilson, B. 1988a. "The Bill W. – Carl Jung Letters." In *The Language of the Heart: Bill W.'s Grapevine Writings.* New York: AA Grapevine.

Wilson, B. 1988b. "The Greatest Gift of All." In *The Language of the Heart: Bill W.'s Grapevine Writings.* New York: AA Grapevine.

Wilson, B. 1988c. "The Next Frontier: Emotional Sobriety." In *The Language of the Heart: Bill W.'s Grapevine Writings.* New York: AA Grapevine.

About the Author

Allen Berger, Ph.D., is a popular recovery author and public speaker. He is an internationally recognized expert on the science of recovery. He is author of Hazelden's *12 Stupid Things That Mess Up Recovery* and *12 Smart Things to Do When the Booze and Drugs Are Gone*. He is widely recognized for his work in several areas of recovery that include

- integrating modern psychotherapy with the Twelve Steps
- emotional sobriety
- helping new patients understand the benefits of group therapy and how to get the most out of it
- helping families adjust to the challenges of recovery

Dr. Berger is also author of *Love Secrets Revealed; How to Get the Most Out of Group Therapy,* a guide for new patients; and *Recovery and Relationship Matters,* a series of eight audio recordings.

Dr. Berger is in private practice in Southern California. You can learn more about Dr. Berger and his work at www.abphd.com.